Joy All Around Us

Joy All Around Us

FINDING JOY IN AN UPSIDE-DOWN WORLD

Written by
Gary Suess, Elizabeth Suess & Tara Suess
Illustrations by Tara Suess

Copyright © 2016 Gary Suess, Elizabeth Suess & Tara Suess
All rights reserved.
ISBN-13: 9780692032961
ISBN-10: 0692032967

Scripture quotations are from BibleGateway.com, a subsidiary of The Zondervan Corporation.

© 1995-2010, The Zondervan Corporation. All Rights Reserved.

Foreword

This book is a unique, collaborative effort of father, mother and daughter—Gary, Beth, and Tara, respectively. Gary serves as the primary author, with the contributions from Beth and Tara that are woven throughout the book identified accordingly. The illustrations are solely the creation of Tara.

Fittingly, creation of the book itself and bringing forth an important message to others was a source of joy for all of them from start to finish. And, artwork is clearly a passion and source of joy for Tara, which in turn, serves to infuse some additional joy onto the pages of the book.

May you experience and find joy!

Contents

Foreword · v

Preface · xvii

Part 1: The Landscape of and Pathway to Joy · · · · · · · · · · · · · · · · 1

Chapter 1 Happiness and Joy ·3

    The Dominos of Grace, Kindness, and Joy · · · · · · · · · · · · · ·3

    Actions, Attitudes, and Choices ·4

    Happiness ·5

    What Is Joy, Anyway? ·7

    The Pursuit of Happiness ·8

    The Good News ·10

Chapter 2 Seeing Blessings, Seeking Joy · · · · · · · · · · · · · · · · · · 13

    Our Blessings, Your Reflections ·13

A Journey toward Joy · 15

A Word from Beth on Collaborative Joy · · · · · · · · · · · · · · 20

Joy from Our Eyes to Yours · 21

Part 2: A Celebration of Joys in Our Lives · · · · · · · · · · · · · · · · · · **23**

Introduction to Joy Essays · 25

Chapter 3 Simple Blessings, Simple Joys · 27

Simply Being Home, by Gary · 27

Tennis, by Beth · 29

Fridays, by Gary · 32

Art Supplies, by Tara · 35

Green Lights, by Gary · 38

Jigsaw Puzzles, by Beth · 40

A Neatly Made Bed, by Tara · 42

Laughter, by Gary · 44

Chapter 4 Blessings of Joy · 47

Skylines, by Gary · 47

Embracing Imperfection at the State Fair, by Tara · · · · · · · · 50

Watching Your Child Perform, by Gary · · · · · · · · · · · · · · · · ·52

Sharing Cherished Memories, by Beth · · · · · · · · · · · · · · · · ·55

Bowling, by Gary ·57

Burning CDs, by Gary ·59

Bird Watching, by Gary ·61

Five Blessings of Joy, by Beth ·62

Departing Church, by Gary ·64

Chapter 5 Joy Here and There ·67

Seasons, by Gary ·67

Oils, by Beth ·69

Conquering a Fear, by Tara ·71

Basketball, by Gary ·75

Discovering a New Artist, by Gary ·77

Finding the Perfect Gift, by Gary ·78

Blankets, by Beth ·80

New Sports Equipment, by Gary ·82

Concerts, by Gary ·84

Chapter 6	Bonds of Joy	87
	Morning Coffee, by Gary	87
	Family, by Gary	89
	Getting Dressed Up, by Tara	91
	Lifting, by Beth	93
	Cats, by Gary	96
	Joy Found in Loss, by Beth	98
	Date Night with Your Daughter, by Gary	101
	Guy Trips, by Gary	102
	Band Encore, by Gary	104
Chapter 7	Kindness and Joy	107
	The Joy of Children, by Beth	107
	Naps, by Gary	109
	Simple Rituals, by Beth	111
	Hanging Around Joyful People, by Gary	114
	A Childlike Sense of Wonder and Excitement, by Tara	116
	Outdoor Dining, by Gary	119

Intentional Acts of Kindness, by Gary · · · · · · · · · · · · · · · · ·121

Life's Little Luxuries, by Gary ·123

Chapter 8 'Tis the Season of Joy ·125

Bonds of Love, by Gary ·125

September Magazines, by Beth ·127

Baseball Stadiums, by Gary ·128

Christmas, by Gary ·130

Listening to Music with Headphones, by Gary · · · · · · · · · ·135

Rebounding, by Beth ·136

Going to the Farmers Market, by Tara · · · · · · · · · · · · · · · ·139

Walk-Off Hits, by Gary ·141

Chapter 9 Sensing Joy ·143

Faith, by Gary ·143

Escaping Monotony with a Bouquet of Flowers, by Tara · ·145

Nativities, by Beth ·147

Food, by Gary ·150

Persevering through Adversity, by Gary · · · · · · · · · · · · · · ·153

Handmade Gifts, by Beth · 155

Blissful Refuge, by Gary · 158

Pizza, by Gary · 160

Chapter 10 Joy Shining Down · 163

Joy under Our Nose, by Beth · · · · · · · · · · · · · · · · · · · 163

Putting a Smile on Someone's Face, by Gary · · · · · · · · · · 166

Rainbows, by Gary · 168

Baseball, by Gary · 171

Sunny Days, by Gary · 174

Winter, by Tara · 177

Seeing Your Child's Gifts Flourish, by Gary · · · · · · · · · · · 179

New Family Member, by Beth · · · · · · · · · · · · · · · · · · · 181

Singing in Your Car Like a Rock Star, by Gary · · · · · · · · · 183

Chapter 11 Joy in Many Places · 185

Gratitude, by Beth · 185

Visiting Your Favorite Vacation Spot, by Gary · · · · · · · · · 187

Sunrises and Early Starts, by Gary · · · · · · · · · · · · · · · · 190

Telecommunications, by Gary · · · · · · · · · · · · · · · · · · · 192

    Heart of God, by Beth ·195

    Retreats to the Wilderness, by Tara · · · · · · · · · · · · · · · · · ·197

    The Next Best Thing, by Gary· ·200

    Trees, by Gary ·203

Chapter 12 Natural Joys ·207

    Plants, by Beth ·207

    True Friends, by Gary ·209

    The Joy of Routine and Structure, by Beth· · · · · · · · · · · ·211

    Joy in Unexpected Places, by Beth· · · · · · · · · · · · · · · · · · ·213

    Hands, by Tara ·215

    Forgiveness, by Gary ·216

    Twins of Different Mothers, by Gary · · · · · · · · · · · · · · · · ·218

    Our Nation—The Gift That Keeps On Giving, by Gary · · ·221

Part 3: Finding Joy in Your Life · **225**

Chapter 13 Deep, Enduring Joy ·227

    Reaching Upward for Joy ·227

    Positioning for Happiness· ·230

    Mentality Matters ·231

Chapter 14 Christianity, Creation, and the Cosmos · · · · · · · · · · · · · · ·235

    Searching for Purpose and Meaning · · · · · · · · · · · · · · · ·235

    The Good News ·236

    Fruit of the Spirit ·238

    No Greater Joy ·238

    Joy from the Lord, by Beth ·239

    Avoiding the Thieves of Joy ·240

    Overcoming Sorrow ·242

    Joy in the Morning, by Gary ·244

    Change, the Enemy of Joy ·246

    God's Five Rs of Relief, by Beth ·248

Chapter 15 Deepening Your Relationship with God · · · · · · · · · · · · · · ·251

    A Deepened Relationship through the Word · · · · · · · · · · · ·251

    The Joy of a Story, by Beth ·252

    A Deepened Relationship through Friendship
    and Intimacy ·254

    Finding Peace Where You're Placed, by Tara · · · · · · · · · · · ·255

    A Deepened Relationship through Worship · · · · · · · · · · · · ·257

Chapter 16 Partnering for Joy—a Match Made in Heaven · · · · · · · · · · ·261

    All Things for Good Testimony ·261

    Walk by Faith, Not by Sight, by Beth · · · · · · · · · · · · · · · · · ·262

    Joy All around Us ·264

    Prayer for Joy ·265

    One Final Testimony ·265

    One Final Wish ·267

Part 4: Finding the Ultimate Joy ·269

Chapter 17 Salvation ·271

    Becoming Sons and Daughters of the Kingdom,
by Beth ·271

    Additional Resources ·275

    Dedication ·277

    Acknowledgements and Credits ·279

    Author Bio ·281

Preface

This book was inspired by the pervasive, lasting joy that I personally came to discover while venturing through my own life journey and the subsequent calling to help others find the same. In an effort to connect and resonate with a broader, more diverse audience, I invited my wife and daughter to collaborate with me by sharing their own experiences, perspectives, and insights.

Our message begins with an acknowledgement of the broken and increasingly upside-down world in which we live. We define happiness and joy, discuss some of our journey, and detail the objective of the book. We attempt to briefly set the backdrop without sacrificing a positive, hopeful tone.

Once the backdrop is established, the heart of the book takes the reader through a series of eighty-four essays that highlight various sources of joy in our respective lives. The tone is intended to be upbeat and lighthearted as well as thankful and contemplative as we fondly detail our experiences and perspectives on the blessings and joys that have graced our lives. We hope that our stories amuse, but at the same time trigger introspection among readers to recognize blessings, recall fond memories, and identify sources of joy in your own lives.

After these personal accounts, the book concludes with specific discussion about the pathways to happiness and joy. Initially, the discussion centers on the ways we can position ourselves for greater levels of happiness through our life choices, mind-set, and influencers around us. Although these catalysts surely promote higher levels of happiness and joy, they also tend to be more temporal in nature, which leads into discussion of the greatest and most sustaining source of joy.

Our book is unique in that it's collaborative in nature, offering varied points of view, all derived from our respective real-life journeys. We hope that readers will readily relate to the diverse experiences, perspectives, and voices offered by ordinary people, and, in turn, that through this connection, the overall message will serve to highlight the absolute attainability of joy in your lives.

There is no denying that this world is full of troubles and sorrow, but fortunately they need not define our lives. We offer our personal testimonies and life experiences to help others overcome those difficulties and ultimately find abundant happiness and joy through situation and circumstance. Our sincere desire is to extend a message of hope and promise to every person who picks up this book that they too can fully discover—joy is all around us!

Part 1
The Landscape of and Pathway to Joy

CHAPTER 1
Happiness and Joy

The Dominos of Grace, Kindness, and Joy

My wife and I recently ventured out to see a movie that we had been anticipating before its release. Our original plan was to battle opening-day crowds to see the local premiere, but circumstances and events put us on a different path. Several weeks later, our schedules and motivations connected to make it happen.

Once we hunkered down in our cushy theater seats and endured what seemed like the ten-kilometer-race equivalent of previews, we were quickly drawn into the feature. While the control room was busy queuing up yet another movie trailer, a young couple and their small son had nestled into the seats immediately in front of us.

As the plot thickened, we got more and more acquainted with this boy, as he enjoyed watching us considerably more than the movie on the jumbo screen. His head frequently popped up over the high-back seats so he could make eye contact, and occasionally he surprised us with his feet wobbling in our faces. This active preschooler was also quite expressive, clearly preferring to be someplace else—perhaps anywhere else.

The movie exceeded our expectations, especially those times when we were able to focus on the cinematography, acting, and dialogue. All in all, the movie was uplifting and inspirational, with a grace-of-God plotline that helped to temper any feeling of frustration.

When the credits started to roll, the theater began to empty. We followed closely behind the family in front of us, winding back through the hallways to the main lobby. As the father headed off to the restroom, we continued to trail the mother and her son until they veered left toward a play area.

Having never looked back until this point, perhaps with thoughts of her son's potentially distracting behavior, the mother seemed very uneasy as she sheepishly gazed up at my approaching wife. Beth made a point of following them to the play area, evoking a look of panic from the woman. When Beth offered friendly words and compliments about her boy, the young mother's fearful look was instantaneously transformed into joy. She happily engaged in conversation and exhibited her innate maternal pride.

This small anecdote highlights our powerful ability to lift the mood and emotions of those around us. Small choices to do the right thing or show kindness, especially when the opposite might be anticipated, often trigger spontaneous happiness or might even make someone's day.

And it may not end there, as acts of kindness and joy can often have a chain effect. It's like one of those videos capturing a long, winding string of dominos tumbling to the ground—only in reverse. Instead of each domino knocking over the next in line, each one rises up and lifts the next, all the way up the line. Perhaps that young mother went on to extend grace or a kind word to someone in the parking lot, her husband, or her son, who in turn did the same.

Beyond triggering this reverse domino effect, acts of kindness can have a very similar effect on the originator. Typically, that is not the initiator's intent, but it is quite often the result.

Simply put, it feels good to know that you took the high road, showed grace, helped someone in need, or simply committed a random act of kindness.

Although we did not discuss how Beth felt on the drive home, she did recognize the positive impact of her actions. Considering the image of the young woman's face lighting up still in my head, I have to think that Beth felt a bit of humbling joy.

Actions, Attitudes, and Choices

As is demonstrated by this brief experience, happiness and joy might result from the actions and attitudes of others around us. Or, these emotions and states of well-being can often come from our own behavior, choices, and perspectives.

Rather than making a snide remark or even offering a disapproving glance about the disruptions and distractions during the movie, responding gracefully changed everything. The boy's mother was clearly feeling uncomfortable with her son's behavior, knowing that others in the theater might not have been enjoying the sideshow, especially those of us seated mere inches behind them. The young parents were walking the tightrope between making an early exit and hopefully persevering to see their blockbuster of choice, which they had already ponied up twenty-five dollars to see, not to mention whatever collateral financial damage was inflicted on them at the concession stand.

We are typically not random "victims" of happiness or joy. These emotions are often a by-product of what we do and how we do it. We can even be very intentional in choosing to live our lives in a way that allows us to experience these feelings more routinely, if not frequently.

Happiness

Happiness is a continuous pursuit for most everyone—from in the moment to an ongoing lifelong objective. For those who are particularly fortunate, happiness may lead to joy.

If we were to camp out on a street corner on any given day and conduct an informal poll regarding individual life goals, it is a safe bet that happiness or some variation would eventually rise to the top of the list.

Although many might cite more specific and immediate life objectives, further probing would likely reveal those as a means to achieve happiness. For instance, someone might wish for their family's well-being, which in turn would elicit happiness. Others might aspire to fame and fortune, but the underlying driver for this goal is the belief that it would make them happy.

Further supporting the notion of happiness being a universal objective, the document that birthed our nation explicitly states this goal at the outset. The most famous and recognizable line of the Declaration of the Independence reads,

> *We hold these truths to be self-evident, that all men are created equal, that they are endowed by their Creator with certain unalienable Rights, that among these are Life, Liberty and the pursuit of Happiness.*

Having the right to pursue happiness and actually achieving it are two different matters, though. There are many traps and obstacles that stand in the way. Even if temporary happiness is attained, sustaining and holding on to it might prove to be even more difficult.

In many ways, we live in an increasingly upside-down world. For many, true happiness is largely elusive, seeming to remain just out of reach. Or, the state of happiness is very temporal in nature. Once the afterglow of an event or situation wears off, the mood heads south.

Every newscast, newspaper, or news feed screams with turmoil. The economy sputters along with minimal growth and underemployment. We seem to work harder for less. Our national debt continues to test its limits like a growing balloon soon to burst. Terrorists continue to multiply and increasingly encroach on our space. Societal divisiveness abounds. Long-standing, foundational principles and values get trampled.

Individually, many of us seek to find happiness by striving and surviving:

- If we do well in school and interviews, we might land a good job.
- If we work long hours and ingratiate ourselves with our boss or employer, a promotion might offer a boost in compensation or greater balance between our work and personal life.
- When the holidays are over, or warm weather comes, or the current demands of life subside, a healthier diet and more intense workout regimen will bring improved well-being or a sleeker physique.
- If we make it through the current rough patch, everything will be better down the road.

You get the idea, and you might very well be able to fill in your own if-then statement.

All too often, the constant demands of today's world have us focusing on surviving. New challenges seem to emerge daily. There are not enough hours in the day to accomplish all that needs to get done. Our to-do list is a bottomless pit. If we can just get through this semester, or complete this project, or land a new job, or get a promotion, or even simply get through the day, we can get to a place filled with happiness.

What Is Joy, Anyway?

Various dictionaries define joy somewhat differently. Some of the phrases used are "great delight," "intense pleasure," "elation," "ecstatic happiness," and a "deep feeling of happiness." Happiness is defined by words such as "pleasure," "contentment," and "satisfaction." *Merriam-Webster's Collegiate Dictionary* defines it as "an agreeable feeling or condition of the soul arising from good fortune or propitious happening of any kind."

Happiness is a fundamental precursor to joy. Most basically, joy is happiness on steroids. It is essentially a greater level of happiness.

Joy is not defined by duration, though. The emotion can be momentary and fleeting, or it can be sustained.

Any number of influences such as events, hobbies, activities, interpersonal exchanges, pursuits, or other physical stimuli can evoke happiness in us. Our level of investment, interest, or passion for whatever it may be, or its magnitude of intensity or success, might elevate the experience to a feeling of joy.

- Winning ten bucks on a scratch-off lotto card might bring happiness. Hitting the jackpot likely moves the needle to joy.
- Meticulously cutting, crocheting, and stitching quilt panels is an enjoyable hobby for many. Proudly admiring the final masterpiece evokes joy.
- Making the play-offs brings happiness. Winning the championship brings joy.
- Getting an A on a quiz makes you happy, but achieving the same grade for the semester might cause joy.
- Getting selected to interview for a new position brings happiness. Landing the job brings joy.
- Helping someone out can make you feel happy. Making a difference in someone's life might evoke joy.

Of course, joy does not necessarily require you to win the state jackpot or the NCAA championship. Joy is often not linked to accomplishments or even tangible things. It is all individualistic and relative in nature. Circumstances matter.

Looking back at the examples above, different circumstances might change the emotions. A lost person without cash or a cell phone finding a winning ten-dollar scratch-off lotto ticket would find joy in being able to pay the bus fare to get home. Cleveland Browns fans might find more joy in making the play-offs than New England Patriots fans. (This is not meant to dis Cleveland, but simply to recognize the context of the circumstances. Not only have the Browns experienced less success on the field, another city once literally snatched the team away from them altogether.)

A struggling undergrad student is going to find more joy in an A than a magna cum laude grad student. The job candidate with five offers will feel less joy in being selected than the job seeker who has been hoping for a breakthrough after six months.

If most people seek happiness in life, living with joy would be the ultimate experience. If you like happiness, you will love joy.

The Pursuit of Happiness

As we journey through life, it is so easy—and normal—to adopt a posture of striving and surviving. The pursuit of happiness becomes the proverbial dangling carrot. We see it ahead, but never quite reach it—or worse yet, someone pulls it away at the last moment like Lucy holding the football for Charlie Brown to kick...or whiff.

We tend to experience happiness as a product of our own striving and current circumstances. As mentioned, this surely poses some problems and pitfalls.

First off, it is extremely hard to always be on the upswing, making things happen and realizing success. Even the best companies, most talented sports teams, and most gifted individuals fall short sometimes, a result that can almost be guaranteed as a by-product of success, which is that the bar gets raised higher.

After the 2013 NFL season, the Denver Broncos lost to the Seattle Seahawks in Super Bowl XLVIII. (That is Super Bowl Forty-Eight for those of you, like me, who prefer a more understated and understandable identifier.) The team began climbing the figurative mountain a couple years earlier, progressing from a last-place team to squeaking into the play-offs before losing. In 2012, the Broncos boasted a 13–3 win-loss record, sharing the league's best mark, before getting knocked off by the eventual Super Bowl champion in the play-offs.

That off-season, the Broncos signed some expensive free agents to shore up their defense, further raising expectations for the upcoming season. The team once again shared the league's top record of 13–3 before winning a pair of play-off games to reach Super Bowl Forty-Eight.

Winning fifteen games and participating in the world's grandest sporting event sounds like a pretty prosperous season. The players, coaches, fans, and entire organization surely experienced much happiness that season, not to mention joy when they advanced to the Super Bowl.

Two days after the big game, the Broncos' coaching staff was let go. The bar had been raised, and nothing short of holding the Lombardi Trophy, awarded annually to the league champion, would suffice. The joy was gone.

Although maybe not on a national stage, most of us experience similar situations. When we hit our goals at work, the goals are raised the following year. When we pass Economics 101, Microeconomics awaits us. Inflation ensures that paying our bills insidiously becomes more costly year by year, if not month by month.

Also, no matter what we do, life brings a steady flow of issues and obstacles that range from minor inconveniences to large challenges. Unexpected expenses, difficult people, illness, economic cycles, job changes—you name it, the next one is just around the corner.

Even worse yet, some try to find happiness in all the wrong places. There is a mountain of empirical and anecdotal evidence (as well as our own gut instinct) to show that these circumstances are a dead-end street, so it is not necessary to expound on the pitfalls of excessive drinking, drug abuse, inappropriate relationships, etc.

If our happiness is defined by our circumstances or achievements, it becomes largely limited and fleeting. Is it possible to string together an ever-flowing stream of happy circumstances or experiences? Can those happy moments reach the intensity of joy? Or, can we accumulate enough happiness to feel joy in our lives?

The Good News
The good news is that there are some ways to influence your overall state of happiness and experience joy beyond engaging in activities that make you feel happy or joyful.

The first involves your approach to life and the expectations that you maintain. In a nutshell, a positive demeanor and outlook tend to produce positive outcomes and experiences.

Mentality matters.

If we expect the worst, we are more apt to get bad things. Conversely, if we anticipate good things, chances are greater that those good things will become reality. It sounds too simple to be true, even bordering on naïve—but not so. Your attitude and outlook influence both how you embark on and how you engage in anything, as well as how you perceive it. That, in turn, leads to better outcomes and greater satisfaction or happiness.

Renowned theologian and psychologist Norman Vincent Peale spent a large portion of his life studying this phenomenon, producing literary works about it and speaking on it. Although he was met with the opposition of various naysayers and nonbelievers, Peale enhanced and even transformed many, many lives through his biblically centered teachings.

A second way to influence your state of happiness is to increase your visibility and awareness of all the good things around you. It is common, and utterly human, to take many things for granted and not recognize an abundance of blessings. Many of these are the fabric in the backdrop of our lives but often fade into the overall scenery and out of our consciousness. In effect, we cannot see the forest for the trees.

Much like those unpleasant surprises around the corner, blessings are everywhere, and we can see them if we open our eyes and hearts.

Really, there is joy all around us.

Another means to stoke up joy is to simply surround yourself with joyful people. Rubbing elbows with upbeat, happy people rubs off. Some of the effect relates to the previous two means, as your attitude, outlook, and recognition of the good things around you are enhanced through positive role models.

But it goes beyond that. Joy is contagious. The glass that was once half-empty suddenly becomes half-full when everyone around you is seeing it more bullishly.

The fourth way is through grace by faith. We will circle back to this later, but there is a reason that joy is referenced 218 times in the New International Version Bible.

CHAPTER 2
Seeing Blessings, Seeking Joy

Our Blessings, Your Reflections

Each one of us is like an original Monet painting, palm print, iris, or snowflake—we are one of a kind. Each of us is a true original with almost infinite permutations of uniqueness, defined by differences in personal attributes, circumstances, preferences, interests, personalities, habits, talents, and more.

We hope that opening our hearts and sharing some of our life stories will touch you in some way and open you up to seeing the world in a different way. We hope that our collection of anecdotes, blessings, and sources of joy offers some comfort, reflection, introspection, and perhaps a few smiles and laughs along the way.

By retrospectively taking you to some of the stops on our respective life journeys, we aim to stoke up some of your own fond memories.

It is our hope that you will increasingly view, or even simply begin viewing, life through a different lens. Instead of being visually impaired by the dark cloud of challenges, tribulations, heartache, and worry, a bright light will illuminate your surroundings to sharpen your visual acuity for the sources of happiness and joy.

Living in a dark cloud, we become blind to the light. Even those who are not enveloped by this darkness might tend to take blessings for granted and fail to recognize reasons to rejoice. If you fall anywhere on that continuum of missed blessings, you are not living life to its fullest. Embracing the blessings and their sources, rebounding quickly from the troubles, expecting good outcomes, and choosing to set our system's default settings to center on happiness will bring us joy and change our lives.

Considering the aforementioned uniqueness of each of our readers, we also hope that we might find different connection points by offering some varying perspectives, voices, and writing styles. As you may have already noticed, this book is somewhat unique in that it is the collaborative effort of three—specifically, our own little family. By design, opposing or varied voices such as masculine versus feminine, corporate versus casual, athletic versus artistic, parent versus child, and young versus "not so young" might resonate differently according to your stage of life, station in life, season of life, personality traits, and circumstances.

These factors also might help to influence our interests and passions in life. Surely, some interests seem almost innate, even partially defining who we are. Some things flicker as an interest early in life and rage into a passion that burns within us for the duration.

Oftentimes, though, our pursuits might align with our age or season in life. For instance, strapping on shoulder pads and a helmet for a gridiron battle might skew toward your more youthful days. Similarly, a working mother with young children might find more time to pursue the arts, golf, or tennis as her children's independence increases.

Or, operating *the* best lemonade stand in town is a more likely passion for a nine-year-old than starting up a new online brokerage firm. That same girl, though, might very well develop a passion for the latter pursuit later in life.

Pitching a nine-inning complete game is clearly no longer in my future. Or, more accurately, pitching is no longer in my future, period. But writing songs and learning to play the guitar are interests that I am pursuing now that my baseball-playing days are behind me.

As is probably common to most families, we have each had very different journeys in life and quite possibly (ha-ha) might not agree on everything. We do have many things in common, but we also harbor many perspectives, likes, and dislikes that are profoundly individual.

For this reason, we feel it is important to tell you a little about ourselves—our journeys, our perspectives, our objectives, our makeup, or simply whatever stuff seems apropos. Although we have often shared the same paths, we have each been on different journeys to get to our current station in life, experiencing the world differently and leading us to varied points of view.

In telling our stories, it is not our intent to raise ourselves up. Here, and in the short essays that follow, we are not trying to say, "Hey, look at us!" in any way. Instead, we hope to provide some backdrop and context for what follows. Then, by sharing the varied sources of joy in our lives, we hope to illuminate the blessings and sources of joy in your life.

Some things may be readily relatable. Others may require some tangential thinking. There may not be a high percentage of readers who were ex-baseball pitchers, but the number goes up when you drop the pitcher qualification. Suspending yourself fifteen feet in the air wrapped into swaths of fabric may present less commonality, but music and sunny days probably capture a high percentage.

It is our desire to hold ourselves not higher, but rather lower. We have received and experienced many blessings—as you may also find as you reflect on your own life. By humbling ourselves to acknowledge the blessings, we are able to see the true source of joy.

A Journey toward Joy

Similar to most people's, my life has been a journey of twists and turns, ups and downs, and forward and backward movement. At times, the journey seemed to figuratively soar above the clouds. Other times, it felt more like a free fall in a tangled parachute. Many times, my life has been like a jet at twenty-five thousand feet and trying to climb, not quite able to get to the prescribed cruising altitude.

Even when the path reached relatively lofty heights, any accomplishments beckoned greater expectations. Flying at twenty-five thousand feet can be exhilarating, unless you or others expect you to be at thirty thousand feet.

Largely, my life has been filled with lots of doing. Of course, for most everyone, normal everyday life presents an abundance of demands and an ongoing supply of to-do-list bullets. In bold print at the top of my adulthood list has always been **Work**, with its own bottomless pit of subbullets.

For most of my adult life, my work life consumed a huge part of my intellectual and emotional energy—not to mention time. Unexpectedly, a couple years out of college, I found myself building and leading a business, launching a career filled with more of the same. Time and events presented different scenarios, scopes, challenges, and demands to keep things interesting, if not nerve-wracking.

Outside of work, I still hungered to play the sports that had been a part of my life from an early age. And when I say that I played sports, I mean a lot of sports. In the seams, I found time for family and friends, although these athletic activities largely involved the latter, and sometimes the former.

Considering the limitations of twenty-four hours in a day and seven days in a week, sleep was often shortchanged. Worse, though, was that family was often shortchanged, as my days and nights were consumed with long hours at the office and then doing other stuff.

As I reflect back, there have been a few major inflection points that particularly altered my life, my family's life, my mentality, and my heart. The first was almost eighteen years ago, when a merger led to my relocation from Pennsylvania to Charlotte, North Carolina. In relatively quick order, we made the decision to accept the new position, and within a couple months, Beth, Tara, and I moved into our new southern abode.

Although it is always difficult to leave family and friends behind, we loved this new southern city that offered urban advantages while maintaining a small-town feel. It was a wonderful experience overall and a great place for Tara to blossom from a five-year-old into adulthood. We immediately settled into our new community, called Ballantyne, and Forest Hill Church, both of which were welcoming and shaped our lives greatly. And, fortunately, we encountered a large number of other transplants, so it was an environment conducive to forging new friendships.

Having left all my sports teams behind and figuratively drinking from a fire hose in my new role at work, I pared down my athletic endeavors to just one sport. I took up tennis, putting softball, baseball, basketball, football, bowling, golf, and volleyball in the past. This allowed more time with my family, but my driven nature still compelled me to invest an abundance of time into furthering my tennis skills and playing this newfound sport.

After a number of years, turbulence started to hit the large bank that brought us to Charlotte. With its stock price chronically sagging, the company started reaching and strayed from sound discipline while looking for ways to meet investor expectations and prop up earnings. This included a horrific, weakly vetted decision to acquire another bank with a mortgage portfolio that was the financial equivalent of a ticking time bomb. It was like being on a plane and helplessly watching as the pilots navigated into an ominous, towering cloud bank—we knew we were going down.

One night, while speaking to Beth via hands-free cellular connection on my drive home, animatedly expressing frustration about the chaos and dysfunction at work, I was involved in a high-speed crash. My all-time favorite car was totaled, but pretty miraculously everyone walked away from the accident with only minor injuries. I briefly lost consciousness after impact, awakening to an airbag in my chest, wipers sweeping frantically, lights blinking crazily, smoke billowing inside and out, and many people lined up on the side of the highway. My last thought prior to that moment was whether I was going to die.

Considering the potentially devastating consequences of the accident were limited to but an array of crushed metal, this situation was undoubtedly a blessing—a major blessing—but also a wake-up call to release the bitterness and anger that had been building inside. It was also a call to find my true identity, examine priorities, and reset my operating system.

A couple rocky years and a major failed acquisition later, our company was forced to sell at a fire-sale price. The bad news was that this led to my departure during a historic meltdown in both the financial industry and the overall economy.

The good news was that this afforded me a great deal of time at home with my family. The workaholic was suddenly a homebody. This continued as I later chose to start up a small business, working mainly from my home office. My commute went from twenty miles to sixteen stairs.

Interestingly, I experienced a sequence of athletic injuries during this same period. Rather than ramping up my court time and amping up my tennis game with the sudden bounty of free time, my tennis game diminished, and my court time dropped off. Surgery put me into physical therapy and my tennis racquet into storage for almost a year. My respective work and recreational lives suddenly disappeared simultaneously.

It may seem counterintuitive for many, but my faith strengthened during this period of adversity and uncertainty—as did my relationship with

Beth and Tara. This period was definitely one of those inflection points where my life course turned sharply upward.

While researching and planning the start-up business, the abundance of newfound time allowed me to throw myself into writing. This had long been a secret passion, dating back to high school, so this period afforded me the opportunity to exercise those muscles for something other than scribing e-mail, memos, strategy documents, and presentations.

Aside from the occasional personal-space invasion associated with my increased presence hanging around the figurative water cooler at home, the additional time with my family surely allowed us to bond more closely.

But it was more than that. My entire view of life was transformed.

Most importantly, I suddenly came to realize how much I had been blessed through my whole life. And, accordingly, how much I took those blessings for granted.

My previous mentality was that whatever I put my mind to, along with my characteristic unwavering, dogged determination, I could achieve success. To paraphrase the caricature-like, smug spokesman for a major car rental company in a humorous commercial, I did not like to think of myself as a control freak, but rather a "control enthusiast." I could figure things out and make them happen.

This proved to be a double-edged sword. On one side, the proof was in the pudding with some arguable results and accomplishments, although I largely didn't even recognize those things as I was always striving to do better. On the other side, there was a growing pressure to make things happen that fell squarely on my own shoulders.

Awakening to the realization that accomplishments were really blessings in disguise was life changing.

Yes, hard work, determination, and ingenuity are still valued traits that contribute to success, but without the right circumstances, favor, protection, God-given abilities, etc., etc., none of the perceived achievements would have happened. Understanding that I was not the true source of success also lifted the burden off my shoulders to figure out how to pull the next rabbit out of a hat as expected by corporate—or by my own driven-to-succeed personality.

Over a couple years, the corporate world continued to come a-knocking (surely more blessings). Eventually, the Homebody Era was replaced with the Nomadic Era when I was lured back into the financial industry.

This three-year whirlwind tour started with weekly flights back and forth to Buffalo for eight months, followed by a brief residency in the uber-cold-and-windy city by Lake Erie. After selling our house in Charlotte, Beth and I became western New Yorkers for about five and a half months, leaving Tara behind at the University of South Carolina.

We actually built a house in "sunny Buffalo," planning on being there for the long haul—or at least the medium haul. On one of the many sub-zero, snowy days served up by the not-quite-great-white-north region, a well-timed text message enticed me to have a call about what appeared to be a great new opportunity back in the southeastern region we had loved. After a couple warm, sunny visits in the South, we were packing up the "Family Truckster" to join a big-splash start-up in Greenville, South Carolina.

The once well-capitalized venture had some hidden challenges and issues. Before long, investors were getting cold feet and the three-year-old company started heading into a descent. Regulators and investors precipitated a dismantling of the company, which led to the sale of the division I headed. A shotgun wedding suddenly had us pointed toward Atlanta, with a plan to relocate once we sold our Buffalo home.

In the interim, I was back to weekly commuting for eight months until a decision to step away from the new company. "Atlanta, here we come" was replaced with "Greenville, home sweet home"—and thus another inflection point.

Besides offering a respite after an incredibly intense three-year journey, this juncture has put me back around the residential water cooler rather than living in another city. Although I may occasionally infringe on Beth's personal space, the net effect has been to further bolster our marriage. The time has also allowed me to get actively involved with our new church (Bridgeway Church), further my spiritual walk, deepen my faith, forge relationships with others outside work, rekindle my love of music, and fire up the literary muscles once again.

Something else very profound also has happened during this period. Through all the déjà vu, *Groundhog Day* adversity and uncertainty, I have experienced a lasting, deep feeling of peace and joy.

The latter, along with some divine inspiration and everything else above, combined to spawn this book. The only missing ingredients were the rest of my family members. Somewhat nervously, I pitched them the idea, and was delighted when they enthusiastically jumped in feet first. With God for you, who can be against you?

> **What shall we say about such wonderful things as these? If God is for us, who can ever be against us?**
> **—Romans 8:31 NLT**

A Word from Beth on Collaborative Joy

Gary had been "threatening" Tara and me for weeks. He had repeatedly told both of us, "I have a business proposal for the two of you." That was the extent of the information we could extract from him despite both of our efforts to question him about this mysterious brainstorm.

Initially he only had an idea, a vague concept in his mind. As I have lived with him for twenty-five-plus years, I know this initial idea evolved and developed in his mind considerably during those weeks of threatening. Until he started to flesh it out by actually putting pen to paper, or more accurately keys to document, however, the true life of this project could not be birthed.

Perhaps partly to build our curiosity and anticipation, but more so due to his attempts to catch us when he believed we would be receptive and open to the idea, Gary held off the unveiling of his idea for over a month.

Exactly one month after his threats began, Tara and I both received an e-mail that began as follows:

Dear Cherished Family,
After further thought and consideration, please accept this as my official proposal for an important family joint venture.

The e-mail went on to describe the overall book concept and alternatives to its development. It detailed the roles each of us might take on as it progressed, and ended with an invitation for a family conference to discuss and further evolve the concept. As I went on to read this two-page correspondence from my husband, I was truly overwhelmed. Thankfulness and excitement filled me as I considered taking on a book project with the two most important people in my life. As I reflect on that day, I recall that joy, the subject of the book, was welling up inside me as I contemplated this adventure.

As I write this now, we are nearing the completion of our book. I personally can say that the process of contemplation of joy these past months has most definitely increased the overall level of joy in my day-to-day life. Not only am I more naturally joyful now than before we started this journey, I am also better able to guide myself to a position of joy as I face "unjoyful" circumstances and events. I can personally attest that this life skill truly reaps huge benefits in the quality of one's life.

It is my sincere hope that the book you are holding in your hands will start you on your own adventure to this end. As you step into our lives via these stories, may our experiences bring a smile to your face and a dose of joy to your heart. And as you end your time with us, may you find yourself changed as well, filled with and strengthened by a greater level of joy.

From our family to yours, joy.

Joy from Our Eyes to Yours

It is easy to understand the word *average* when used in conjunction with numbers. Three threes and a seven average four. Even with the newest "new math," no matter how you get there, the answer is pretty clear cut.

When used in terms of describing a human life or person, though, the calculus is much more nebulous. What does it mean when someone says, "We are average Americans" or, "We have lived average lives"? Can that be reduced to a certain income range, career choice, family size, religious belief, or any other factor? How would an equation even be formulated? My math-oriented brain could surely take a crack at it, but the methodology would be so subjective, the output would be rendered pretty meaningless.

As mentioned earlier, we are all unique like snowflakes or fingerprints or golf swings. With that in mind, I will refrain from trying to do the math to see if our little family falls within the defined range to be considered average.

Although it's unclear whether we are average, what is clear is that we offer our individual life stories in the context of being on a fairly normal, ordinary path. We are not celebrities of interest. We do not have particularly unusual or compelling backgrounds that will keep you on the edge of your seat or provide a story of tremendous conquest and inspiration.

But that's the point.

We may be a lot like you in many ways—or at least in some ways. Even if our likes, passions, and collective journeys are different, there are likely many parallels. At a minimum, the emotions may be very much the same.

It is our hope that our utter ordinariness makes us even more relatable—and thus an inspiration. If we were rock stars or famous politicians or all-star athletes, the promise and hope of our book might be lost in the notion that it is attainable for only those relative few at the pinnacle.

Most importantly, happiness and joy are equally available to each of us. These states of being are not defined by wealth, or fame, or prestige.

We all stumble. We all face challenges, lows, and highs. We all have circumstances, actions, and plenty of other stuff that we don't want posted on our Facebook page. We all have figurative skeletons in our closets.

The good news is great news. Joy is available to each one of us. Sustaining joy is not only possible—it is there for the taking. Every one of us can have it.

We truly offer both our backstories and the joy stories that follow with sincerity and humble hearts.

We hope they spark some emotions in you. We hope they stir up some of your own good memories. We hope they shine light on the blessings and sources of joy within your own life. We hope they bring some smiles to your face and maybe stoke up some outright feelings of joy.

Part 2
A Celebration of Joys in Our Lives

Introduction to Joy Essays

The following ten chapters that comprise part 2 of this book provide a collection of essays collaboratively written by our small nuclear family: Gary, Beth, and Tara—father, mother, and daughter. Each musing has been inspired by our respective life journeys, offering our unique perspectives and insights into particular sources of joy that graced those personal expeditions.

We offer this array of memories, observations, and experiences accompanied by an intent for sincerity, vulnerability, humility, appreciation, and gratitude. You will likely find the assemblage both diverse and random, ranging from very personal to universal and lighthearted to somewhat weighty in nature.

This collection of musings is offered not as a celebration *of* our lives—but rather as a celebration of the blessings and joys *in* our lives. Surely, the eighty-four topics covered here do not represent the sum total of the joys we have encountered through our lives. Instead, these are the ones that emerged in our thoughts as it came time to put fingers to keyboard over the past several months. This is in keeping with our book's premise, particularly when we proactively position ourselves for those purposes, that joy is all around us.

Our desired objective is threefold as you work through this section of the book. First, it is our aim to entertain and amuse through our personal reflections—and perhaps even to conjure a bit of joy in the moment. Next, we hope that our stories might be relatable, triggering your own fond memories and recognition of things around you that provide happiness and joy. Lastly, we hope that the exercise of saturating your mind with a wide-ranging variety of joys will stimulate greater introspection and contemplation, leading to an overall greater awareness of blessings and joys in your own life.

CHAPTER 3
Simple Blessings, Simple Joys

Simply Being Home, by Gary

Our family has been on quite a journey the past three years. We have moved five times, bouncing from three cities spanning across a six-state area in the eastern United States. During that period, I also often found myself living away from home four to five days per week.

Besides getting new licenses, reregistering cars, filing multiple tax returns, tracking down missing mail, and countless other little associated tasks, being unsettled became the new norm. This is not all bad, as it really brings home how great it is to simply be home!

Sometimes, until you are without something or living on the other side of the fence, you do not really appreciate simple blessings in life. This is not to say that a traveling salesperson or professional athlete cannot find happiness while spending a great deal of time on the road, but I am guessing that, like me, they truly better appreciate the comforts of home.

For the first seven months of this journey, I lived out of a suitcase—albeit a very large one. Each week, I would pack up with the precision of a US Navy SEAL, fly off to Buffalo, and return home five days later. This provided a brief window to launder clothes and repeat the cycle once again.

> I can distinctly recall the feeling of anticipation that would envelop me as I awaited the return flight, and then the excitement that would rise within me as I drove home from the airport. I was usually dead tired after a trying week, but the adrenaline pumped me up and put a bounce in my step.

It was déjà vu all over again when I recently performed a similar dance to another city for eight months. Although this time it was close enough to avoid air travel and a heavy parka, I would feel that same unmistakable feeling of excitement build as my car got closer to home on the three-hour drive.

Arriving home was always extra special when I was greeted at the door knowing that "absence makes the heart grow fonder" on both sides. Of course, it was better for me, as I was regaining the comforts of being surrounded by our own stuff and sleeping in my own bed.

As a famous fictional character in red shoes once proclaimed, there is truly "no place like home."

**The ache for home lives in all of us, the safe place
where we can go as we are and not be questioned.
—Maya Angelou**

Tennis, by Beth

My father owned and operated a hardware store until I was about fifteen years old. Above the hardware store, we had two apartments; our family lived in one, and my grandmother lived in the other. On the back side of the business, where we entered our apartment, were four garage bays and a loading dock. Behind the building was a parking area, and beyond that was our lawn, which surrounded the back and one side of the building. I describe this scene not only to paint a picture, but also to illustrate how different it was from an average suburban home complete with a picket fence and yard.

When I was about seven, my father decided he wanted to take up tennis and converted our parking lot into a tennis court. He quickly convinced the entire family to join him in pursuing this sport for the first time in our lives. Although all of us were beginners to the game, it was a fun family activity that provided hours of enjoyment. Soon my father had lights put up around the court so we could play well into the night hours. Many evenings were spent with friends and extended family joining us for some friendly competition on the court.

Although my passion for tennis started in my backyard, it did not really take root until much later, when I was an adult and our family moved to Charlotte, North Carolina. Tara was six years old when we settled into a family-friendly southern neighborhood that had a tennis center and a thriving tennis program. Here I started taking lessons and soon found myself on a tennis team with my neighbors. Tennis not only provided a way to get some exercise, but it fostered friendships as we competed against other local clubs for the seasonal trophy. During what I like to refer to as my obsessed phase, I was playing tennis for two hours each day, or more.

Many women who enjoy tennis will also admit to the joy that comes from collecting a fun tennis wardrobe complete with hats, shoes, and bags. Each year our club would offer us new team "uniforms." In reality they selected a line from one of the tennis manufacturers, so we had many different styles to choose from but always in colors different from the previous year's. Despite the fact that we knew this practice was mostly about the club making money, most of us happily indulged our shopping genes and picked out an outfit or two so we could coordinate with our teammates in the upcoming season. Somehow, stepping onto the court in a cute outfit has a way of increasing the joy factor.

Since we moved away from Charlotte, my tennis pursuit has significantly cooled, despite the fact that we reside in a tennis-friendly climate and are members of a tennis club. I briefly joined a tennis team at our new club but found that my limited time was turning a stress-reducing activity into a stress producer. Sometimes the route to more joy in one's life is making the tough decisions on what to keep and what to let go. Currently my tennis activity consists of weekend hitting sessions with my husband. We both enjoy keeping our skills up, getting some exercise, and indulging in a bit of friendly competition as well.

As the responsibilities in my life change, I'm sure there will be a time when I will once again pursue tennis in a more formal way. Belonging to a team is a unique bonding experience that is hard to duplicate in other arenas of life. Winning a hard-fought tennis match for your team produces a huge shot of joy. Conversely, losing a tough-fought match can strengthen resolve and remind us how to be a gracious winner. Being able to celebrate others' victories is a good sign that you are pursuing and embracing a joy-filled life.

For now, I am very content to enjoy my limited trips to the courts, as I get to do it with my best friend. And as a bonus, it allows me the opportunity to wear some of my cute tennis outfits.

JOY ALL AROUND US

Fridays, by Gary

There is something about Fridays that is inherently happy. Somehow, your mind and body seem wired into them it subconsciously. They literally occur like clockwork—as does the sense of joy that radiates inside of you.

Without even peeking at your smartphone to remind you of what day it is, there is a special feeling in the air when you wake up on Fridays. And it seems to carry throughout the day.

What makes it even more special is that not only do you feel it, but so do most people you encounter. That internal sparkle tends to take the mad rush out of the frantic, fast-paced world around us. Rush hour traffic is a little less tense and a lot less aggressive.

Fridays bring quick smiles and laughter, even when circumstances might stir up a frown or frustration on other days. Anxiety and anxiousness you may have been feeling earlier in the week seem to release into the air like a balloon with a loosely tied knot. But unlike the balloon's inevitable drop to the ground, you defy gravity and remain emotionally soaring.

Time seems to slow down, allowing you to enjoy everything around you a little more.

The last day of the traditional work and school week provides an unmistakable shot of energy. Human batteries are recharged, and a current seems to flow through the air, making Fridays electric.

There is a reason that no one coined the phrase "Thank God it's Wednesday!" or "Happy Thursday!" Although, as this book attests, there are abundant reasons to feel happy and joyful every day of the week, Fridays are universally special.

Surely, there are logical explanations for the magic of Fridays.

As mentioned, for most, the freedom and relaxation offered by the weekend are on the way. It is interesting, though, that this special feeling occurs on a business day rather than an actual weekend day. Perhaps that speaks to the promise and hope of what is to come, rather than the actual events.

Although probably never studied, the propensity for donuts to show up in the break room must increase exponentially on Fridays. Besides the obvious appeal of this unexpected culinary treat, this phenomenon highlights the increase in magnanimity that naturally occurs on this particular day.

Paydays typically fall on Fridays—surely an inducement for happiness. The hoopla of high school football and basketball games traditionally falls on Friday evenings. For many, the evening events get stretched further into the night with the privilege of sleeping in the next day.

Families often realize the opportunity to spend time together after a hectic week of everyone running in different directions. Friday evenings are also a time for socialization with friends. Sometimes, the night simply provides an opportunity to shut down and relax after a taxing week.

But for all the tangible reasons for your mood to soar on Fridays, we seem to carry an inner sense or subconscious awareness that drives these emotions. From the moment you awaken, you feel an extra bounce in your step, and a sustaining smile forms in the corners of your mouth. Thank God it's Friday.

Art Supplies, by Tara

One afternoon, I overheard one of my colleagues talking to another about how much she loved opening a brand-new box of crayons. "ME TOO!" I butted in and exclaimed with perhaps excessively genuine enthusiasm.

"Weirdos," my other colleague teased.

What's better than a brand-new box of crayons? I wondered. There's the array of beautiful colors, the unmarred, perfectly molded, pointy tips, and the distinct, waxy smell. Then, most importantly, there are the endless creative possibilities.

I remember, as a child, collecting numerous boxes of crayons over the years. I distinctly remember always going through the red much quicker than the other colors, and I remember the perils of an important crayon breaking in half or the sharpener becoming jammed and dull.

I also recall owning a very special box of Crayola crayons. They were vintage, limited-edition "collector's colors" that came in a sturdy tin instead of the standard yellow-and-green cardboard box. I kept the tin on the shelf in my closet, where it would collect dust until I'd decide to take it down to look. That was all I did—look, never use. They were too special to use. I would simply open up the box, marvel at the colors—seventies-schematic colors with interesting names—and then close it back up and put it away.

As an adult, I still have boxes of Crayola crayons lying around in my apartment, and purchasing a brand-new box is still just as exciting, if not more so, for nostalgia's sake. But I have also grown into more "mature" art supplies.

Upon taking a painting class in college, I learned how to select and make oil paints and how to mix primary colors to make any shade I desired. I learned how to work with encaustic, watercolors, pastels, and ink. I've since begun a vast collection of "adult" art supplies that range from oil paints to watercolors, from illustration markers to smooth ink pens. Bringing home new art supplies remains equivalent to opening up that new box of crayons to an extent.

The difference, though, which perhaps makes the experience of purchasing new art supplies even better, is that with expensive, professional art supplies, you can rarely purchase all seventy-two colors at once. Each purchase requires mindfulness and tact. If I could run out and buy a three-hundred-piece marker set for twenty dollars, that'd be *lovely*, but it would also be a bit mundane and eliminate the excitement of building a cherished collection. Instead, when I peruse my local art supply store, I know that I can only leave with no more than five markers at a time, and I know I must choose wisely. I am required to build my collection slowly, ensuring that each color is selected with care and is well worth the number on its price tag. If that makes me a weirdo, then I'm a happy weirdo, and I think that's just fine.

JOY ALL AROUND US

Green Lights, by Gary

We have all experienced running late. Your heart thumps a little bit faster, rhythmically seeming to bump against your rib cage.

Whether we're rushing to work, school, a medical appointment, a social gathering, a job interview, or some other type of event, that uneasy feeling of anxiety rushes over us at the point that we realize we are cutting it very close. Even worse yet, our internal calculations and navigation system may be giving us a figurative thumbs-down.

Although it almost never feels good to arrive late, with the possible exception of an occasional "fashionably late" appearance at a party by design, the level of angst is proportionate to the importance of the appointment. Much like the moments when you awaken from those recurring dreams of forgetting to study for a final exam, your heart races while your body tenses up.

Some days, you may have forgotten to set your alarm, or perhaps you hit the snooze button once or twice. Or there are days when you cannot determine a suitable ensemble, or you get sidetracked with another matter. Traffic might be particularly voluminous or snarly due to the weather or for no discernible reason. It could simply be due to someone else being late or slowing you down.

The causes can be many, and no matter what, they sound trite and meaningless when conveyed to others. Dentists, school principals, and prospective employers have undoubtedly heard every "the dog ate my homework" story imaginable—and perhaps some others that rival *Seinfeld* episodes in terms of creativity.

And when the calculus to get from point A to point B seems greater than the time you have available, your mind searches to formulate how to explain your tardiness. Saying, "I just couldn't drag myself out of bed this morning," does not invoke a very favorable impression and rarely rolls off anyone's tongue. Of course, making up some lame story is surely not right either. Many times the explanation will be translated as "My time is more valuable than your time, so I thought it would be better for you to wait than me."

Usually, the best way to handle tardiness is to simply say, "I'm really sorry for being late." Fortunately, there are sometimes days when, against all odds, everything breaks your way.

Specifically, what comes to mind is when, like the parting of the Red Sea, you somehow hit all green lights on your drive.

Early on, you happily avoid the harsh glare of red on the yellow fixtures hanging above. After getting the timing right on the next couple intersections, you start to sense your run of luck and wonder if it can continue. Again, more green lights, and the anxiety begins to dissipate.

You are now in the home stretch, and you blurt out, "Please don't change," as you see more soothing green ahead. You notice an amber warning glow above just as your rear bumper scoots through the intersection. At this point, you recognize it is feeling a lot less like a lucky streak and more like divine intervention.

When you arrive at your destination, that queasy, anxious feeling has shifted to a sense of joyousness.

You just dodged the proverbial bullet, and you won't let this happen again—or so you convince yourself as you happily check in.

Jigsaw Puzzles, by Beth

If you could see a picture of my childhood living room in the winter, you would find a card table set up in the corner holding a jigsaw puzzle in process. If my memory serves me, soon after the Christmas decorations were boxed up, the card table would make its annual appearance. It would be positioned near a floor lamp for maximum lighting, and chairs from the dining room would be gathered around as needed.

Sometimes the puzzles were new, with pieces accompanied by dust from production gathered in the box corners. Sometimes the puzzles were purchased at flea markets or yard sales; they often had the picture somewhat obscured by a homemade price tag. A less than perfect visual of the project could be overlooked, but the main concern with used puzzles was whether or not the box contained all the pieces. The answer to this concern would only come once the puzzle was completed.

My mother was the champion of puzzle assembly in our home. Almost every night, sometime after dinner, she would take her place at the card table and spend time "working," as she called it, on her puzzle. I don't believe my dad ever joined her in this interest. He would be in his chair, our dog sleeping next to him, happily watching TV or reading a book. Just reflecting on this family memory brings me joy.

I guess you could say that in the puzzle-making arena, I was a bit of an amateur. I liked the initial excitement of a new project and the promise of creating something, but I was somewhat less than diligent during the whole process. I especially liked the beginning, looking for all the edge pieces and finding matches as the outline took shape on the table. Once the outline was complete, which can be accomplished fairly quickly, and the harder work began, my interest would wane. Most nights I would spend only minutes at the table.

My mother toiled away alone, occasionally mumbling under her breath that there must be a piece missing. As the puzzle neared completion, my interest would start to increase again. I am not sure if it is because the act of finding the correct placement for a puzzle piece gets increasingly easier the further along you are, or because I just like the excitement of being there for the big reveal. I imagine it is a little bit of both.

Although I didn't receive the puzzle gene from my mother, miraculously it skipped a generation and was implanted in our daughter, Tara!

Even without possessing this gene, I had collected puzzles as an adult with the hopes that one day their completion would provide us with special memories, a source of joy for our family. I still remember when I witnessed Tara's possession of this gene. We were visiting family in Pennsylvania, and my mother gave her an old puzzle. She attacked that thing with a persistence that put my mother to shame. She was determined to finish it before we packed up to head home, and she did.

The puzzle given to her on that family visit did provide us with family bonding time as all three of us worked together toward a common goal, just as I had imagined. Since then we have enjoyed putting more puzzles together as a family. I still start out strong, disappear for a while, and then return for the big reveal. Thankfully Tara understands me, and I am content in knowing my mother's puzzle gene lives on.

A Neatly Made Bed, by Tara

I can be a bit nutty about my bed. No matter how many times I hit the snooze button, how much my beauty routine will suffer, or how many minutes ago I should have *already* left for work, I don't ever leave the house without making my bed.

It's laughable, because I wasn't always this way. Growing up, the only time my bed was made was if the sheets had been washed that day. Otherwise, it remained in a constant state of disheveled disarray.

I began routinely making my bed in the morning as a proactive measure. I've found, personally, that a neatly made bed makes all the difference in my mood and productivity. Although the state of my bed couldn't matter less while I'm away at work all day, when I come home, I need to be able to dig in and focus.

You see, I don't work my nine-to-five and then come home to eat spaghetti and ice cream in front of the television (as lovely as that would be). I come home, and there is always more work to be done. Not paid work, but side projects—things I do to build the career I *want* to have, not the career that I currently have.

So, when I return home, remove my coat, and toss my shoes in the closet, I need to be greeted by a pristine bed. I need to return to a tidy room that says, "All is okay. Stay sharp. Stay focused."

If I return home to a messy, unmade bed, I might as well just turn in for the night. It's sort of a Zen thing—I'll personally take on whatever aura my bed exudes. Thus, if my bed is tidy and organized, I will feel tidy and organized. If my bed is a disheveled mess, I will feel like a disheveled mess.

While it could perhaps seem a bit strange that my productivity is so dependent on something as trivial as the state of a bed, I love having the ability to make such a huge positive impact on my mood with such a little, simple thing.

Then, the most rewarding part of a neatly made bed is the process of unmaking it at night, when I've toiled and deserve a good night's sleep.

It's like staying in a hotel every single night. I toss the throw pillows on the floor, plump my regular pillow to the perfect density, and snuggle between sheets that have been so tightly tucked I feel like a baby being swaddled. I swaddle myself in my bed, and everything is okay. I can let go of the stress of the day and relax.

JOY ALL AROUND US

Laughter, by Gary

Can you imagine a world without laughter? I can't.

A world without laughter would be dark, dreary, depressing, mundane, and almost lifeless. It would be like summer without sunshine. It would be like food without flavor.

There is a reason someone coined the phrase "Laughter is the best medicine."

Although this is not a quotation from the Bible, it surely finds its roots in Proverbs 17:22, which says, "A cheerful heart is good medicine, but a broken spirit saps a person's strength."

Laughter is a very powerful force in our lives. It lifts us when we are sad or in the dumps. It moves us past anger or annoyance. At its most basic level, it is deeply intertwined with what we experience as fun. If you had a fun experience, laughter was likely a small part of it—if not all over it like intense brilliance on the sun.

When I contemplate the interrelationship between laughter and joy, it brings to mind the age-old question, "Which came first, the chicken or the egg?" When you reflect on it, laughter and joy in many ways present a circular equation.

We laugh when we find words or circumstances funny. We laugh when something makes us joyful.

On the flip side, laughter can make us joyful. Those who are light of spirit and quick to laugh surely find joy to follow.

Joy brings laughter—and laughter brings joy!

Similarly, sometimes, if we are bold enough, we laugh in the face of danger to pump ourselves with courage. It allows us to put the situation in perspective and maintain a sense of calm to deal with whatever is causing our blood pressure to rise and our hearts to race.

Reflecting back on your own experiences, the most enjoyable and memorable social gatherings typically were not rooted in an evening of debating quantum physics (not that there is anything wrong with mathematics or photons, headache aside). More likely they were those evenings when you hit the sack with your gut still hurting from raucous laughter all night and woke up the next morning with a smile still affixed to the corners of your mouth.

Of course, laughter does not need to be that extreme to impact our mind-set and emotional state. It can come in small doses throughout every day.

Possessing the ability to see humor in almost any situation or circumstance is truly a gift. This can be especially true if the target of the laughter is yourself or your own circumstances. Although I am not advocating developing low self-esteem, it seems apparent that laughing at yourself (or whatever hand you have been dealt) now and then provides great benefit.

Virtue can be found in not taking yourself too seriously. Besides keeping you humble, it can push you past the darkness of sadness, self-pity, anger, or even depression. Borrowing a bit of wisdom spoken by that noted maven of human behavioral science, Ronald McDonald, laughter "turns a frown upside down."

Negative emotion turns into positive emotion. Unhappiness becomes happiness—leading you to a neighborhood on the outskirts of joy. In other words, where there is laughter, joy might be right around the corner.

Our mouths were filled with laughter, our tongues with songs of joy. Then it was said among the nations, "The Lord has done great things for them."
—Psalm 126:2 (NIV)

CHAPTER 4
Blessings of Joy

Skylines, by Gary

Like snowflakes, although man-made, no two skylines are alike. If you gaze past the forest to the trees, each skyline offers a unique assemblage of shapes and angles. They impose crisp, straight lines to complement the infinite, free-form permutations of nature.

The shapes and dimensions of each collective city skyline tend to serve as a living barometer of a city's attributes, growth, vitality, and creativity. A more expansive footprint that reaches higher into the sky typically signals a larger population, but the elegance and artistry of the design might reflect the heartbeat of the city.

Vibrant, growing cities are more likely to display newly built structures commingled with bright lighting and rich colors. Metropolitan areas with an engaged constituency and vision for the future tend to exhibit an integrated rationality within the overarching design rather than a random smattering of rectangles. These groupings of buildings tell a story beyond the collective cityscape they form.

For reasons beyond my immediate grasp, it became clear to me at an early age that I love skylines.

Somehow, it has always stirred joy within me to marvel at these unique architectural complexities. This was true when our family passed through any city when I was young, and it remains so today, many years later. This speaks to why I prefer a window seat when flying, enabling a real-time, aerial view of the cities that I am visiting. If I am lucky, I may also catch a glimpse of other skylines on the journey.

Perhaps there is some ancestral branch that connects me with Frank Lloyd Wright, as I have always experienced skyscrapers as works of art. This would tend to explain the extensive array of skyline paintings and photographs that have adorned the walls of our homes through the years.

Fortunately, my wife embraced this little obsession of mine from the start. I am not sure if she sees the artistry as well, or if the percentage of our art collection that falls within this genre simply means many will make the cut to be displayed. My speculation is that there is at least a subconscious appeal since she does not shut down the idea of looking for local art when we visit new places—which inevitably translates to cityscapes or other architectural images.

If I were to imagine being stretched out on a couch answering probing questions from an intensely thoughtful, bearded gentleman with a notepad, it might dive into my heart and mind to touch on the roots of this fascination and how it evokes feelings of joy.

Beyond the artistry, it seems that each building represents a substantial accomplishment, involving many contributors. Every individual structure contributes to the whole but in and of itself represents a triumph of many.

Each tower requires research, detailed planning, precise engineering calculus, thoughtful and optimally creative design, pencil-point-sharp financing, political influence, meticulously orchestrated organization, selfless collaboration, a wide array of uniquely skilled construction workers, and a mountain of concrete and steel. And let's not overlook tremendous courage, from taking on such an expensive endeavor to being ominously tethered thirty stories in the air as the blueprints turn into a structure.

It literally takes a village to build a city.

At the most fundamental level, city towers are *the monuments of man*. They reflect our progress from the days of mud, straw, and blunt instruments. They represent the power instilled and infused in our minds and bodies by our Creator in heaven. Cityscapes symbolize mankind's ingenuity, hard work, strength, and determination.

These constructs of brick, stone, concrete, and glass represent strength—both in terms of physical stature as well as the collective population that lives and conducts business in each metro market. As the daylight yields to darkness, they provide an elegant beacon of light shining brightly in the sky.

Although I might not have comprehended this cognitive reasoning as I first gazed upon these collections of man-made artistry towering in the sky, it seems clear why they have continued to fascinate me. It makes sense why these images adorn our walls. And it seems clear that walking past these wall hangings, and ultimately being surrounded by the real thing, evokes a little bit of joy.

Embracing Imperfection at the State Fair, by Tara

"If we do anything this fall, we have to go to the fair," I begged my roommate at the start of October, none other than prime fair season and my favorite month of the year. "If we can't go apple picking, carve pumpkins, bake a pie, or go to a Halloween party, that's all fine, so long as we go to the fair."

Luckily, she obliged.

Attending the fair each fall is important to me. It's an integral component of the autumn season, a must-do in my book. I'm not exactly sure when the fair became an object of my affection, as I didn't grow up attending fairs or carnivals with my family, but it managed to win my heart sometime during my young adulthood.

Going to the state fair is kind of like reaching your hand into a mystery toy box; you never really know what you're going to get. Sometimes it's slam-packed with people waiting hours to get on a single ride or to get their hands on an oily funnel cake and a sweet caramel apple. Other times it's cold and rainy, and you discover that you are one of only ten groups of individuals who are dedicated enough to attend a fair in the rain.

Sometimes you're harassed everywhere you turn: "Step right up! Three chances to win big!" Other times you're able to disappear into the crowd to the extreme of almost immediately losing track of your entire group of friends: "I swear I only turned around for five seconds!" Sometimes a llama spits on you, the elephant you're riding stops abruptly to "use the restroom," or a ride breaks down after you had finally advanced to only three deep in line. Sometimes the fried desserts make you ill, and oftentimes you're forced to wonder what it would be like to be a traveling carnie or one of those racing pigs.

I think it's the imperfectness of it all that makes attending the fair such an interesting cultural experience. You don't go to the fair thinking it will be an exceptionally clean and highbrow experience; that's what the ballet and opera are for. You go to the fair expecting a little bit of dirt and grime, exceptionally terrible-for-you fried foods, and some good, cheesy, deep-in-the-belly laughs and fun. You expect the imperfection, which is something we probably don't do often enough.

Sometimes we need that. Sometimes we simply need some good, hearty fun that doesn't require a masking layer or seriousness or expectations. At the fair, I can ride the Ferris wheel, play some silly dart-throwing games, pet a few docile animals, and eat my once-a-year serving of fried Oreos in a friendly space where all are welcomed and all walks of life are represented. At the fair, I can expect the unexpected and simply enjoy the imperfect, goofy nature of life.

Watching Your Child Perform, by Gary

It happened more than five years ago, but I can still clearly recall how I felt as I drove home. Somewhat unexpectedly, my eyes teared up as I started up my car and headed out of the parking lot.

The moment occurred after watching our daughter play her last high school tennis match. Her senior season was over—and so was her career. Tara was heading to a large university and had no plans to further pursue tennis competitively.

The reason that this was a melancholy occasion for me is that watching her play provided me joy—much more than she ever knew or could really appreciate.

It is not totally clear why this was the case, on either front. From her standpoint, she was just playing a sport, and it was not that big of a deal. For me, perhaps the emotions were somewhat innate as a parent, but there must be more to it than that.

As a little backdrop, I have been a sports junkie my entire life. If I wasn't competitively playing myself, I was watching a large array of sports. As baseball, basketball, football, volleyball, and fast-pitch softball became more of a physical challenge as the years advanced, I took up tennis.

Tara was always more of a girlie girl and interested in the arts such as music, art, reading, and writing. It became apparent early on that she and I would probably not spend a whole lot of time throwing or hitting a ball around together.

The one exception was tennis. She started taking lessons as a four-year-old, before I did. When I would sneak home early from work to watch her lessons, it seemed that she was amused, but not in love with playing the sport. As a competitive sports lover, I found that disappointing, but I still wanted her to pursue the things that made her happy.

It was a bit of a mild (albeit pleasant) surprise when Tara decided to try out for the high school tennis team as a freshman. I wasn't sure what to expect, but it became apparent that somewhere along the line she may have received my competitive gene. The coach had set up a challenge-ladder system to let the players sort things out themselves on the court, and Tara was determined to play her way onto the team.

She succeeded and found herself making her way into the lineup. The following three years, Tara was firmly planted in the lineup, reaching number two singles on a team that was state ranked. She demonstrated a remarkable fighter's spirit on the court, frustrating her opponents by relentlessly returning their best shots. It is important that she always did this with good sportsmanship and integrity.

Perhaps I was simply a proud dad appreciating his daughter demonstrating tenacity to succeed. Perhaps I was thankful that she gave me a chance to see her compete in sports. Perhaps it was those things and more, but I do know that it made me very happy to watch her. I would also imagine other parents share those same sentiments, whether it's tennis, golf, dance, basketball, or whatever the chosen passion.

Sharing Cherished Memories, by Beth

When I was a little girl, my mother would tell me about her many paper dolls, describing them to me in detail and recounting how she played with them for hours. Just as I was very excited to introduce Barbie to our daughter, my mom must have wanted to pass her love for paper dolls on to me and my two sisters. As I was the youngest, with a considerable age gap between me and my siblings, most toys that were once their prized possessions were generously passed on to me. This understandably included paper dolls.

I can't say that I remember actually playing with the paper dolls per se, but I do remember them being a part of my childhood. I recall the slight frustration of having to wait for my mother to cut out a newly purchased set when I was very young. As I waited, I would page through the book admiring the pretty outfits, hoping soon she would sit down and say, "Okay let's cut these out for you now." I remember cutting them out very slowly and carefully when I was old enough to wield scissors for myself, yet still, inevitably, cutting off a tab or two in my excitement.

Often the dolls came with a folder that could be used to keep them safe and unbent. Even as a child, I was particular about organization, and keeping things neat and tidy was important to me. Most of my paper dolls, however, did not come from the store but from my mother's magazines. For the few of you old enough to remember, you know immediately that I am referring to Betsy McCall from the ladies' magazine *McCall's*. Not every month, but fairly often, this magazine would contain a page with Betsy dressed for the appropriate season, including two additional outfits, all color coordinated and ready to be cut out and enjoyed.

Unlike my siblings, with no one to pass my treasures down to, I kept many of my paper dolls into adulthood. I still have a collection that includes some from my childhood and some I have found as an adult. These new acquisitions remain uncut but still somehow give me a bit of that childhood joy when I review their glossy pages.

After unpacking from our last move to South Carolina, I came upon the box containing my collection of paper dolls. I sent a picture of the oldest set, the Lennon Sisters, which had belonged to my sister Debbie, to both of my sisters as I was unpacking. They were excited to see this childhood memory. Soon after, Debbie advanced the idea of making copies of the Lennon Sisters dolls and outfits so we all could have one. I knew immediately I wanted to return them to their original and rightful owner.

Fairly soon after we were settled in our new home, a visit from Debbie and her husband, Jim, was planned. I was very excited to give her this gift, so I wrapped the large ziplock baggie containing the Lennon Sisters and all their outfits in a gift bag and set it aside for their arrival. On the first day of their visit, as we enjoyed a beautiful spring day on our screened porch, we exchanged gifts. When Debbie found her childhood paper dolls inside that gift bag, she smiled, and then she cried, then she smiled and cried some more. You get the picture. The emotions tied to childhood treasures can be very precious. What a blessing for me to be able to return this treasure to her. And perhaps that day, as adults, we got more joy from those paper dolls than ever before.

Bowling, by Gary

Like my parents, my grandparents bowled regularly in leagues, but they also took it a step further and competed in semiprofessional tournaments. As a result, I was exposed to the sport at an early age, when socks had to substitute for overly spacious bowling shoes.

It was also my maternal grandmother who turned me on to watching the *Pro Bowlers Tour* broadcasts. I looked forward to tuning in every Saturday afternoon to watch the culmination of each weekly tournament.

Those broadcasts developed my fascination with learning to spin those sparkling, artistically crafted, sixteen-pound balls with expert precision to destroy the pins dutifully waiting on the other end of the alley. It became apparent to me that bowling required a unique combination of strength, hand-eye coordination, mathematical calculation, and rote muscle memory. A key to success, after sizing up the shot, was to take your head out of it and allow your ingrained muscle memory to execute.

The greatest delight in bowling came from developing the exact blend of speed and spin to consistently guide the ball into the "pocket" in a way that would cause the pins to explode into the air before all falling to the ground. Rotation, velocity, accuracy, and angle acuteness of the ball cranking into the pocket all merged to define success.

My bowling career officially launched as soon as I reached the minimum age to join a junior league. Saturday morning bowling became part of my weekly ritual and quest to hone my game. After high school, my bowling ball mostly went into hibernation through college and a few years following, before I was enticed by my father and friends to join their team.

My one cameo appearance was when I tested out to receive required gym class credits in college—one game, pass or fail, based on exceeding a score the instructor thought unreachable. Little did he know about my more than decade-long clandestine passion for the sport.

Fortunately, when I resumed my career with my father and friends, the muscle memory was still there and took up right where I had left off. Even more importantly, our Monday night league provided a boost to the beginning of the work week and rekindled my love of the game. It was an absolute bonus that I got to enjoy the time with my father.

For me as an adult, the sport presented a bit of a dichotomy in my life. Bowling did not always fit the boardroom persona that was expected of me in the business world. For that matter, neither did playing fast-pitch softball. Thankfully, I did not let that deter the copious joy that I derived from participating in these sports.

The country-club golf set, prone to wearing pastel whale-patterned pants with matching polos, tended to view bowling as a conduit for drinking beer with the guys. Similarly, the tennis set tended towards its conservative underpinnings of white-on-white tennis outfits and the politely competitive demeanor of Wimbledon, judging bowling as not quite a *real* sport.

Mentioning my affinity to bowling inevitably conjured up the image of me wearing one of those ugly short-sleeved, button-front shirts along with a pair of clownish multicolor leather shoes. Although I can say that I have never owned a bowling shirt, I am not a bit sheepish to own my identity as a bowler. I was okay being the odd duck. And, for the record, beer was not part of my bowling experience.

After several years, my bowling equipment once again returned to storage when we relocated to the Southeast. It has been many years since I last stepped on the alleys, but my past experience suggests that my muscle memory remains intact, awaiting the next invitation to join a team. Considering that I do not know any bowlers within a five-hundred-mile radius, it could be a long wait.

Perhaps the sport is in the DNA of my familial ancestry, or perhaps it's just an acquired taste. Regardless of the reason, I just know that it has provided many hours of enjoyment in my life.

Burning CDs, by Gary

If you are like me, music lifts your spirits, energizes you, invites deep thoughts, and simply makes you happy. It can make the difference between a boring gathering and a great party, success or failure in a sporting event, or perhaps even a good or bad decision.

Technology has made it simple to assemble your current favorite songs or those of a similar genre into playlists customized just for you. Oftentimes, I find myself creating playlists that combine songs that hit me a certain way, such as pumping me up to push through a workout, creating a digital mood ring, bringing me closer to our Father, or putting a smile on my face.

When I find the right combination of songs, that playlist tends to provide countless hours of enjoyment, energy, and positive thought. It seems only natural to want to share that playlist with others who mean a lot to you.

Burning a CD with your favorite playlist is a good-faith attempt to bundle some of your joy onto a little plastic disk for someone else to experience the same. It is an overt, tangible way to bestow best wishes on them.

Unfortunately, we are all very different, with varying preferences, likes, and dislikes. The songs that you love and that speak to you might not land on everyone else the same way.

But that's okay…even in that case, it is the thought that counts. You just hope that the recipient will at least give the CD a once- or twice-over to discover whether they might find the same level of inspiration or joy.

I would say it's worth a couple hours to listen. Giving your special playlist to someone else can itself be a source of joy.

Bird Watching, by Gary

My wife has long had a passion for watching birds. This either originates in Beth's DNA or is a love and appreciation that was taught by her father in her childhood. I suspect it is both.

My father-in-law possessed a deep love for nature. He chose to spend as much time outdoors as his work schedule and other responsibilities would allow, drinking it all in and marveling at God's creations. He studied even the smallest details very intently, developing an ever-expanding knowledge of the laws of nature and God's order.

It was also his passion to share that passion with his own children and their children. As I would watch him walk our daughter around pointing out different species of birds or types of trees, I gained a window into my wife's upbringing.

Those same walks through the yard or the woods in the park clearly nurtured my wife's love for watching birds. She can quickly identify the species and type within visual range. She also gets bonus points for identifying other types nearby according to their gleeful chirps.

These are skills that I do not possess, as my outdoor time through much of my life involved focusing on a variety of sports balls. Unfortunately, watching the spin of a curveball, the rotation of a football, or the bounce of a tennis ball detracted from my awareness of the nearby wildlife. For this reason, I appreciate her knowledge and have allowed her to get me up the curve over the past several years.

This education coincided with Beth's decision to create a mini bird habitat by placing a bird feeder in our backyard approximately ten years ago. It was all fun and games until the squirrels assumed control of the feeder and then proceeded to conquer our attic. After professional help and several thousand dollars of repairs to resolve our squirrel problem, the backyard bird sanctuary sadly ended for Beth.

We recently moved into a new home with a deep backyard. After careful contemplation and calculation, Beth quietly dusted off the bird feeder, dragged it into the exact right location, and set up shop once again.

Any sunny morning now, you can find her gleefully watching the ever-growing number of birds that have found our little sanctuary. A couple weeks ago, she took it to the next level when she asked her sister to send her a pair of her father's old binoculars.

It is hard to tell who is happier—the birds or Beth?

Five Blessings of Joy, by Beth

Currently we have five furry blessings in our home. Most people would be able to easily identify them all as members of the cat species; to us, however, they are much more than cats or even pets. They provide us with daily doses of joy and laughter as well as bring additional life into our now two-person household. My husband, Gary, often comments how different our home would be without them, and I couldn't agree more.

In the summer of 2013, we unexpectedly lost one of our blessings. Adidas, who was normally a very happy girl with a big appetite, stopped purring and stopped eating. I took her to the veterinarian within a day of these changes and expected to have a prescription issued to get her back to her normal self. As I waited in the examination room for the doctor to bring her back and provide news on her condition, it seemed just like one of my many, many visits to animal hospitals.

The doctor returned to the room without Adidas and said something to me that I initially was not able to comprehend. On reflection, it was not the terms she used that confused me but the unexpectedness of the question she was asking. "Adidas is going into cardiac arrest. Do you want us to resuscitate her?" As I realized what she was saying, my thought and response was, "Yes, of course!" *Please save my baby*, I added inwardly to myself. Sadly, Adidas was already gone. She would not be coming back to the examination room, and I would be taking her crate home empty. Not a normal trip to the veterinarian, by any means.

The loss of Adidas was very hard for all of us. She had a larger-than-life personality that personified sweetness. Her big, blue eyes always looked a bit cross-eyed, which gave her a perpetual quizzical look, and the slight curl at the top of her tail added to her cartoon-style cuteness. She was also a bit overweight…Truthfully she was fat, and we affectionately nicknamed her Fatty. She wore it so well, however, that her fatness made her even cuter. It was not surprising that the Facebook page I set up for her was well received.

This tremendous loss compounded with the loss of my mother a year earlier, and together with the stress of our multiple moves, it threatened to pull me into a dark place. Thankfully God had a new furry blessing waiting in the wings that would help heal my heart.

> **You have turned my mourning into joyful dancing. You have taken away my clothes of mourning and clothed me with joy.**
> **—Psalm 30:11 (NLT)**

Departing Church, by Gary

Life is short, but I find myself increasingly looking forward to "next Sunday." Although Sundays typically entail some of my favorite things—namely watching football or baseball, playing tennis, quiet family time, relaxing, and good food—the highlight of each week is attending church.

There is something particularly powerful about gathering with family, friends, and neighbors to worship and hear the Word of God. It gets a quick jump start when the band breaks into a song permeated with moving music and lyrics, followed by a message that somehow speaks directly to each and every person.

We have been blessed to find an amazing church with leaders grounded in the Word and empowered by the Holy Spirit. Regardless of the current circumstances, I find it almost impossible to depart each week feeling anything less than energized and uplifted.

When it is time to depart, a truly special feeling of joy has ballooned within me.

It is quite apparent that others are feeling exactly the same way as smiles, laughter, warm interactions, hugs, and words of encouragement are everywhere to be found. As we head to the parking lot, I find my mind racing and my heart beating a little faster than when we arrived.

Although I am certain my wife shares a very similar experience and feeling, it is also apparent that it may trigger different reactions. My brain typically races from topic to topic, and I want to openly talk about each thing that comes to mind. This is almost always powered by the joyousness I feel.

Sometimes, my wife wants to do the same. Other times she is still processing and reflecting on it all (which likely makes my chatter quite a distraction).

Regardless of how the experience manifests itself on any given Sunday, there is no doubt that our bodies and souls are rejoicing. For us, church is like one of those little smart-car stations popping up in parking lots everywhere—we depart with our batteries fully charged for the week ahead.

> **Splendor and majesty are before him;
> strength and joy are in his dwelling place.**
> **—1 Chronicles 16:27 (NIV)**

CHAPTER 5
Joy Here and There

Seasons, by Gary

Most of us tend to navigate through life simply accepting the laws of nature without giving much thought to the technical mechanisms and machinations behind them. Although we covered many of these topics at some point in our scholastic careers, once the exam was over, the knowledge of axis tilts and rotational synchronicity likely dissipated into the atmosphere like the smoke of a distant fire.

Yes, there are those science geeks who cataloged the knowledge for a potential guest appearance on *Jeopardy!* or simply to feel more in touch with the universe around them—but my guess is that most are simply content with knowing that the law is as predictable as dropping a bowling ball on your toe and do not stress about being put on the spot to explain it to a room full of their toughest teachers in high school.

Accordingly, the average American just needs to know that it is becoming time to pull the sweaters and parkas out of storage. Or, they know that bathing suit season is right around the corner, so a couple extra workout sessions each week and a salad for lunch now and then might be wise choices.

But somewhere between putting away the golf clubs and explaining the winter solstice to a fifth grader, there is an array of marvelous phenomena that add richness to our lives. That is surely true of the annual seasons.

Depending on where you live, these seasons may be more or less pronounced. If you live at the equator or one of the poles, four seasons feel a lot like one. However, if you were to live in, say, Washington, DC, you would experience four distinct seasons over the course of 365 days.

Now, at this point, I know some are saying to themselves, I could do without the cold, messy winter weather—or perhaps the opposite: summers are just too hot and humid for them.

For me, personally, spring and summer are my favorite times of the year. The smells of flowers, shrubs, and trees blooming and fresh-cut grass trigger happy memories of baseball season. The spring offers the soothing pastels and joy of Easter, followed by the temperate, sunny weather that stirs an anticipation of summer.

Summer means pool parties, vacation excursions, amusement parks, ice cream, and barbeques. And, perhaps through our conditioning as youth with the extended school break, there is just something magical about summer that carries through all our metaphorical seasons of life.

It is hard to argue the appeal of spring and summer, but when I reflect on it, I would not want to give up the other seasons.

Fall brings colorful foliage, the mad frenzy of football season, trick-or-treat sugar highs, crisp morning hikes in the woods, and the Thanksgiving holiday to count your blessings and unabashedly consume upward of five thousand calories with loved ones in a single sitting.

Despite the cooler temperatures and abundant darkness, winter offers the most celebrated holidays of the year—Christmas and the New Year! Winter also brings snowmen, ice-skating, basketball season, festive decorations, and roasting chestnuts around an open fire. (I threw that last one in for poetic appeal. Does anyone really light a pile of wood to hang out and cook nuts?)

Activities and events aside, would we even appreciate spring and summer the same way if not for the dark and cold of winter? A little challenge always makes success that much sweeter.

All four seasons bring joy—each on its own terms. Although winter and spring host the most joyful holidays of the year, the warm, sunny weather and abundant activities still give summer my nod for the most joyous season overall.

> **They celebrate your abundant goodness
> and joyfully sing of your righteousness.
> —Psalm 145:7 (NIV)**

Oils, by Beth

I'm sure most people would agree that olive and coconut oils are unusual sources of joy. I agree in theory, but my daily infusions of joy from the use of both of these oils cannot be denied. I'm sure you are well aware of the many uses of both oils, and as such their versatility is certainly part of the allure. For me, however, they are more than useful products; they are an integral part of my day, one that I would certainly miss.

Let's start in the kitchen, where I consume olive oil multiple times a day. It is a healthy fat, the experts tell us, and I love the taste. For me, finding a food that is both good for your body and that pleases your palate has to promote joy. I put olive oil on my toast for breakfast, my salad for lunch, our roasted vegetables for dinner, and popcorn for my late-night snack. I also consume coconut oil multiple times a day, but more indirectly, as I use it for cooking. Before my eggs, vegetables, and even some meats go into the pan, they are treated with coconut oil.

I have both a second bottle of olive oil and jar of coconut oil in my bathroom. I use the olive oil nightly to remove my makeup and occasionally as a moisturizer. I use the coconut oil as a moisturizer as well, both on my face and body. Coconut oil is both antifungal and antibacterial, so if I have a cut or suspicious sore, I slather on the coconut oil. Both oils also work great as hair masks and cuticle treatments. Multipurpose is definitely their middle name!

Sometimes the joy from these oils comes in unexpected ways. Recently, when faced with a double door that was sticking and hard to open, I had the offhand idea to put olive oil on it. Presto—problem solved. The door now works better than when it was first installed. I have used olive oil many times to stop doors from squeaking and coconut oil one time to fix a broken zipper. I am almost to the point of throwing olive or coconut oil on any and every issue as a first resort. Olive oil is part of my cleaning arsenal as well; I use it on stainless steel appliances as well as for the removal of errant sticky substances.

I am not the only member of our household who believes oils can be a source of joy. Because Pippa (one of our *five* cats) can't talk, we need to rely on her actions to decode her true feelings. Every evening around nine thirty, Pippa heads into our bathroom and settles in on my vanity stool.

If I enter the room, she is sure to make her presence known with a few meows. As it gets later and I come in to get ready for bed, she starts pacing back and forth on the counter. She continues pacing and soon adds meowing to the mix as I brush my teeth. The vocal reminders and back-and-forth dance continue until I give her what she wants. I can almost hear her say "at last" as I open my jar of coconut oil and scoop out a taste for her to enjoy. I can't remember when I discovered she has an affinity for coconut oil, but one thing is for sure: she is relentless in her nightly pursuit of this unique treat. Although this little ritual is now part of our routine, I still smile every time, and the joy from this small scoop of coconut oil spills over from her onto me.

People often say joy is found in the simple things, and I believe that statement holds a lot of truth. Savoring an ice cream cone on a hot day, getting lost for hours in a good book, and climbing into bed after a long, hard day all speak to this statement. For Pippa and me, one of those simple joys is found daily in our oil-filled bottles and jars.

> **You love justice and hate evil. Therefore, O God, your God has anointed you, pouring out the oil of joy on you more than on anyone else.**
> **—Hebrews 1:9 (NLT)**

Conquering a Fear, by Tara

Throughout my childhood, I was enrolled in various sports and activities in order to figure out what I was good at—to determine where I belonged.

I found it pretty easy to determine where I didn't belong. I lacked the grace and attention span for ballet, I wasn't about all the slipping and falling associated with ice-skating, and attempting to read sheet music was like attempting to read Braille in Japanese.

When I was five, I gave gymnastics a shot. I didn't totally understand the purpose of learning gymnastics, but it was quite fun. I ran through a spongy pit, I climbed over foam obstacles, and I practiced my balance on a beam with cushy mats below to catch my fall. I'm innately inflexible, but I learned how to stretch, and I learned how to execute a somersault. It was nice to be permitted to run around, giggle, and simply be a crazy preschooler.

One afternoon in class, we were presented with a bar. We were each to be lifted up by one of our instructors, and with her assistance, we were to learn how to flip over the bar. I watched as a few girls and boys ahead of me successfully completed the flip. They seemed unfazed by it, most walking away with smiles plastered on their faces.

I had no reason to be afraid, so I stepped up to the bar when it was my turn. I remember there being a large American flag hanging on the wall behind the bar. And then, I remember that large American flag suddenly being upside down. Disoriented and afraid, I kicked my legs in a panic and cried to be put down. At that point, gymnastics was out.

Fast-forward to the present day, about eighteen years since that terrifying afternoon. With the encouragement and mild persuasion of a friend, I purchased a Groupon to try out a thing called "aerial silks." Think Cirque du Soleil; think those acrobats in leotards who climb, twirl, and suspend from pretty white silks attached to the ceiling. My friend, Kayla, had already been to a couple of classes and assured me that it was very safe and very fun. I decided to give it a shot.

On my first day of class, Kayla advised me to wear tight clothing and a shirt with sleeves. Shoes didn't matter, she said, because we would be barefoot. She also advised me to arrive early, as I would have to fill out paperwork and sign liability waivers, which is always a comforting thought.

Yoga pants and sleeves in check, I pulled up to a windowless warehouse with shabby wooden steps and a small parking lot littered with cracks and blemishes. There was just a tiny sign pasted to the front door indicating that I had arrived at the correct location.

I could turn around and go home, I thought for only a second before ascending the creaky stairs.

Inside, I found myself in a gymnast's paradise. There were ropes to climb up, springy boards to jump from, foam obstacles to vault over, and giant mats to stretch on. Then there was the most aesthetically pleasing area, a row of rainbow-colored silks dangling from the twenty-foot ceiling. Each silk was knotted on a hook attached to the ceiling, the tails cascading all the way down to the floor.

I signed the waivers, tucked my shoes in a wooden cubby, and did my stretches and jumping jacks as instructed. The instructor seemed nice, and she looked like the silks, her hair dyed in a rainbow gradient of purples, greens, and blues.

After warming up, our instructor walked down the row of silks and tied each one. She twisted the ends into a knot at about chest level and informed us that we would each be "flipping in" for that day's class.

Flipping in?

"What we'll be doing today is a little bit more advanced, but I'll break it down, and we'll take it step by step."

Advanced?

I wiped my palms on my leggings and watched our instructor as she demonstrated the moves we would learn that day. It was beautiful and graceful, and she made it look easy, tugging, and pulling, and twisting, and dangling from a neon-green silk.

"But let's just start with the flip-in first. That's your starting position for a lot of moves, so it's important to get it right."

We were to wrap each "pole" of the silk around our shoulders as if we were wearing a backpack and then grab hold as we flipped backward. The result was inverted suspension, like a handstand without your hands.

I waited until the rest of the class had successfully completed the flip-in, studying, scheming, and eyeing the door, before timidly approaching a magenta silk on the end. I slipped the poles around my shoulders, wiped my palms again, and pushed myself backward.

JOY ALL AROUND US

I think my body was only horizontal to the ground when I pushed myself back to upright in a panic.

"Uh, you're not quite there yet," the instructor said. "We'll have to try that again."

It was then that I remembered gymnastics class eighteen years ago. History was repeating itself. I remembered the shame and humiliation of being too afraid to flip over the bar in gymnastics, and I realized I had two choices: I could accept the shame and humiliation again and walk right out the door, or I could do what terrified me, conquer my fear, and learn something new. The decision was obvious.

You just have to do it, I silently scolded myself. *No excuses.*

I said a quick prayer and leaned backward again, this time with the instructor coaxing me to continue rotating until I was completely upside down.

"You can let go now. The silks will hold you."

I reluctantly let gravity take my arms and looked upward to press my palms against the gray carpet. It was a surreal, strange experience, feeling the blood rush to my head and seeing the world capsized.

Before that moment, I had never hung upside down before. Never from dangling on a bar, never from hanging on a monkey bar, never from doing a handstand. Never.

That day, I did something seemingly trivial—hanging upside down—but that simple activity has acted as a catalyst for further stepping out of my comfort zone. That day allowed me to conquer a fear that has plagued me since preschool; it showed me the fruits of not allowing my fears to control me.

Practicing aerial silks was such a wonderful experience, which I would have missed out on had I given in to my fears and walked out that door. I'm so thankful that I didn't.

> **For God has not given us a spirit of fear, but of power and of love and of a sound mind.**
> **—2 Timothy 1:7 (NKJV)**

Basketball, by Gary

Although I currently need to look in the rearview mirror of life to recall the experience, playing basketball brought me an abundance of joy for many years. Besides shooting an occasional shot when presented the opportunity by a friend's driveway hoop or a gymnasium court, it has been a long time since the days of playing organized basketball or even pickup games.

Sometimes when I reflect on the reality that the days of playing sports such as basketball and baseball are behind me, it gives me a tinge of disappointment and nostalgic sadness. The reason for these emotions seems pretty simple—these were such a big part of my life and provided a great deal of enjoyment. These were also team sports that created many friendships as well as a bond with teammates united for a common purpose.

From an early age, an affinity for sports rooted in me and became part of my identity. Certain sports, such as basketball, baseball, and football, jumped to the forefront in terms of appeal, and others followed from there. Considering that a basketball, baseball, or football was an almost constant fixture in my grip, my hands seemingly molded to them as I grew. Along those lines, it was a big day when I was first able to palm a basketball in one hand like some of my favorite NBA stars.

It is unclear when I fell in love with hoops, but it was probably a couple years after the other sports due to the circumferential challenge presented by this large orange sphere. I made up for any lost time by adopting basketball as a year-round sport—by covertly dribbling in the house, sinking baskets across various rooms thanks to the brilliant invention of Nerf products, shoveling off snowy basketball courts, frequently trolling for pickup game within a ten-mile radius, and shooting hoops in our make-shift backyard court.

Although I probably launched more shots there than all the PGA members combined over the entire history of the tour, our backyard court was not ideal. Our driveway was not conducive to a traditional basketball setup, so creativity and my love for the sport prevailed. The basket was mounted on the side of the garage, with a small square of concrete beneath it that once supported a sandbox. The rest of the "court" was grass with, shall we say, abundant and varied topography.

In retrospect, this unusual setup honed my hand-eye coordination and shooting touch, but perhaps left my ball-handling skills a little behind. The challenge of executing cross-over dribbles and spin moves in the grass spawned three-point-range accuracy.

My basketball career stood the test of time, including playing in rec leagues, on school teams, in summer leagues, and then in various organized leagues and forums for fifteen years after college. Smattered in between were countless pickup games.

Even though it is a distant memory, I can still recall the rush of energy during pregame warm-ups with a crowded gymnasium, music pumping in the background, and adrenaline coursing through my veins. It felt joyful.

When not on the court, I was also a devoted spectator of the sport. As a Philadelphia 76ers fan, I was very fortunate to witness some terrific players and great teams. Beyond having to speak with a raspy whisper for a few days afterward, the noise and excitement at Sixers-Celtics play-off games and the Big East tournament burnished lasting memories.

My personal favorite fan moment was sitting in the second row behind the basket where Dr. J performed his gravity-defying reverse layup around the backboard against the Los Angeles Lakers in the NBA finals. Yes, that shot—the one they show during the introductory highlights leading into the current NBA finals broadcasts. Seeing it live, ten feet in front of us, was stunning and makes the word *spectacular* seem inadequate. What a blessing to somehow score courtside tickets and then witness one of the all-time great players invent the impossible in the moment.

On one hand, basketball is simply an odd collection of rules that involves bouncing a ball and tossing it into a metal hoop mounted on a hanging rectangular board. On the other hand, for some reason, it has provided me countless hours of happiness and joy.

Discovering a New Artist, by Gary

Have you ever "discovered" a new band or singer? There is a finite number of performing artists in your music library or on your favorites list—until you discover the next one again and again!

Music is like that, as it is really infinite in nature, mixing unique voices, different instruments, new lyrics, and endless permutations of notes. Songs are the distant cousins of snowflakes and people. No two are alike.

There are myriad reasons why you might like a particular song or performing artist. Perhaps the lyrics speak to you, or the bridge is catchy. Perhaps you particularly enjoy someone's vocal tone and quality. Maybe you get lost in the power guitar chords or the percussion. Perhaps the song takes you back to another place or puts you in touch with certain emotions.

Or it could be all of the above. You probably do not even reflect on exactly what makes the music appeal to you, but one thing is certain—you know it when you hear it.

I have loved music all my life and sometimes reflect on what the world would be like without it. It brings so much color and richness to our lives, yet how often do we step back and view it as a tremendous gift?

Finding a new favorite tune surely brings a smile to your face and puts a skip in your step—perhaps over and over again. When you find a new favorite recording artist, you have hit the jackpot!

> **Sing to him a new song; play skillfully, and shout for joy.**
> **—Psalm 33:3 (NIV)**

Finding the Perfect Gift, by Gary

Over the years, the holiday shopping habits of my wife and me have gotten a lot more alike, but there was a time when they were widely different.

In the earlier days of our relationship, Black Friday would launch me onto an obsessive mission to find the perfect gifts for my extended family and close friends. There was a certain pressure that came with this obsession, which often meant that I would still be out searching days, or even hours, before Christmas Day.

There is no doubt that I spent inordinate amounts of time on shopping excursions, searching every retailer within a reasonable circumference of my home and office. Of course, this leaves open to debate whether a ten-, twenty-five-, or fifty-mile radius might be reasonable.

In my case, a fifty-mile radius was within reason, even when we resided in a harsher region prone to cold and snowy conditions. As the days advanced toward Christmas, my internal clock amped up the pressure.

This little obsession took hold of me prior to knowing my wife. It later became even a little more challenging, as Beth's birthday falls in early January. This was like doubling down, as I quickly learned that I needed to cover both occasions during the holiday season because pickings were slim afterward. (This does not even touch on the fact that she can be a bit of a tough nut to crack, but that is a story for another time.)

Beth has found my gift-giving obsession anywhere from amusing to annoying. There were times that she hoped for me to be at home rather than traipsing all over the map from mall to mall. I must say, there were many times when I felt exactly the same way.

Perhaps she did not totally understand that all of this was driven by my desire to find the perfect gifts for everyone. Of course, perfection was not realistic, so I was often shooting for "I really like it."

Having a loved one react with pleasure from receiving a gift gives me a great sense of joy. That was the case then, and still is now, but my methodology has gravitated toward my wife's approach over the years. The Internet is a great thing!

This is not to suggest that she didn't care about finding the right gifts—it was just a matter of how she went about it. A large majority of my shopping today is online, powered by wide availability, timely shipping, and free returns.

I still find joy in finding the right gifts for everyone—it's just that I now have a lot more time to do other things, like enjoy the holiday season!

> **And I have been a constant example of how you can help those in need by working hard. You should remember the words of the Lord Jesus: "It is more blessed to give than to receive."**
> **—Acts 20:35 (NLT)**

Blankets, by Beth

The love of blankets in various forms is something children find at a very young age. The blanket may be as small as a bandana or big enough to cover a twin bed. It is almost always indispensable, at least where sleep is concerned. Our daughter, Tara, had found her favorite sometime before she turned two. Her blanket was actually not a blanket at all, but a cloth diaper. This came about because we always had one on hand to shield our clothes or wipe up messes. I imagine to her it must have seemed like a part of us, as it was always there.

At some point these diapers' purpose transitioned from cleaning to something more personal and comforting. She began to take them with her as she became mobile, and eventually they acquired the name "Nana." Although we didn't plan it this way, having multiples of this precious commodity was a blessing. Another was always available, clean, and ready to comfort Tara if Nana was lost or in need of washing.

As she got older, Tara must have caught on to this, as the last Nana in existence, now resting in storage with other childhood castoffs, is far from pristine. It is really not a blanket in any form, just a few shreds of its former glory.

Although I don't remember my childhood blanket, you might be surprised to know that now, as a grown woman, I have one. As I prepared to write this, I brought it up with my husband, Gary, to get his thoughts on the matter. He said he just goes with it, and more importantly, he knows that it is off limits. That's a good man!

Like Tara, I slipped into the world of blanket love gradually. The purchase of a Hello Kitty blanket was just because I am a bit obsessed. At some point, the blanket found its way to our bed for a nap or at bedtime, and I found it comforting. Soon I was sleeping with it next to my face every night. And eventually it acquired the name "Face Blanket"—clearly not the most original name I have imposed on something. Now I sleep with it every night and don't even think of the absurdity of it at all. I guess joy is often found in unexpected places, and sometimes the best thing to do is just go with it.

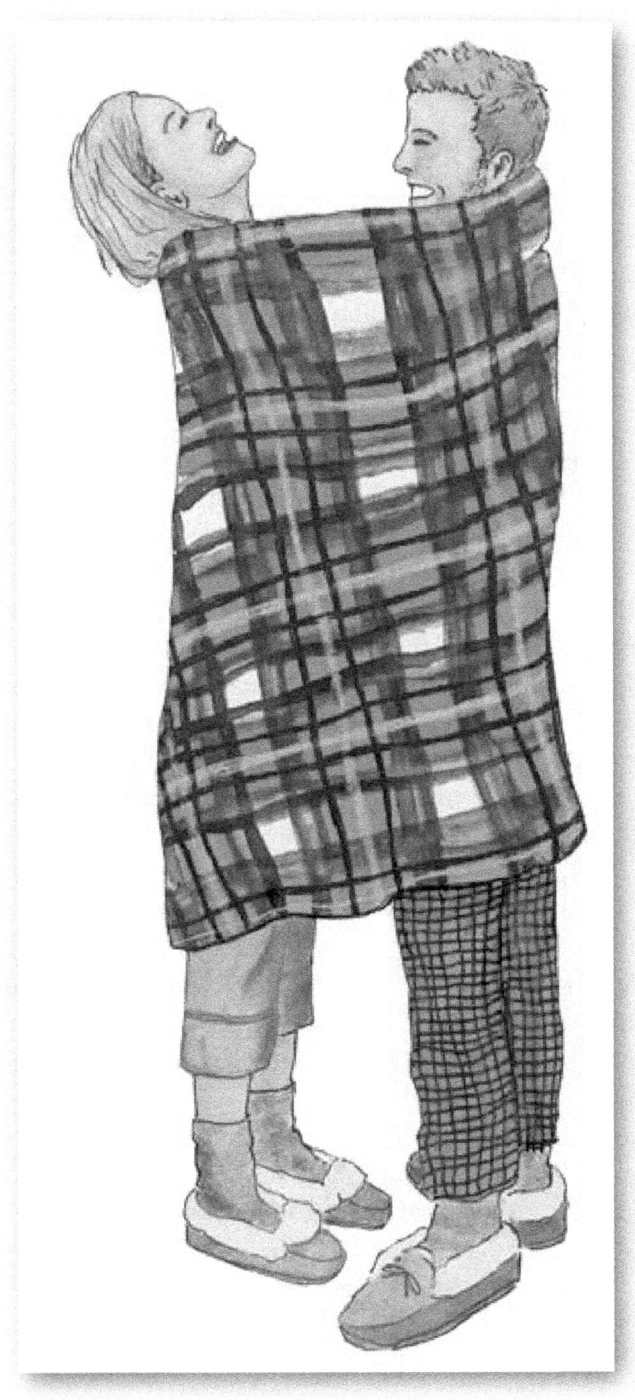

New Sports Equipment, by Gary

After all these years, the memory still vividly sticks in my mind. The occasion was my tenth birthday.

Our family rose early (with a little bit of prodding) to open birthday presents before I headed off to school on this bright, sunny day in May.

I had asked for one specific gift and could not wait to see if my parents might grant me the wish. That season I made the jump to the "majors" in Little League, and I was hoping to be equipped with a new baseball glove.

To my great delight, my parents came through with the new glove that I wanted—a first baseman's mitt just like the one used by my favorite Major League player. Although my ten-year-old hands were still significantly undersized for the massive new mitt, it was instant love!

To give you a couple visuals, the glove was bigger than my head with my hat on. When I would catch a ball in the webbing, I often had to do a double take to make sure it was actually still there.

From that point on and throughout the baseball season, my new glove was a regular companion, sometimes by necessity and sometimes by design. A new glove requires somewhat of a bonding process to mold it perfectly to your hand and properly break it in to maximize dexterity, so it spent an abundance of time with me. The mitt also resided next to me when I slept—just because.

Actually playing was the best, but simply having that glove on my hand gave me joy. To this day, the smell of a new leather baseball mitt oddly conjures up happiness.

Similarly, grasping a baseball or football is a stress reliever and gives me good feelings. As proof, a baseball permanently sits on my desk at home and at the office to grasp and flip while on calls. I try to refrain from that activity when working on the computer or meeting with someone face to face, but you will notice that statement is a little open ended. Although not documented through scientific means, flipping the baseball likely knocks ten points off my blood pressure.

There was a time when I also kept a baseball bat next to those desks for occasional imaginary swings or to take in the fragrance of the burnished maple or ash. It seemed that having a bat nearby was a little daunting to others, though, so I have since reluctantly retired that practice.

No matter your sport, there is something invigorating about holding a new piece of equipment in your hands. It's a bonus if you have success actually using it.

Concerts, by Gary

Although my collective life tenure now allows me to measure time in decades, my passion for music has followed me through those spans of years. This passion is in terms of being a consumer rather a performer. Of course, I sing songs constantly and still do occasionally dream about learning to play electric guitar or figuring out how to unobtrusively interject a drum set into our home décor.

My word selection is very intentional when describing my current relationship with music. It transcends listening and crosses over into consuming. It is not a passive endeavor, but rather participatory in nature. Beyond singing along or playing drums on the nearest hard surface, the lyrics and melodies pour into me, speak to me, and lift my mood.

Considering all of this, the live experience of a concert is extra special to me. An audible experience becomes heightened by both the visual stimuli and the osmotic excitement of the crowd. There is nothing like watching your favorite musicians with a few thousand other rabid fans.

More than anything, music brings me joy. Experiencing it live takes it to the next level.

While some can get stuck in the past recycling the music from their glory days, I am still driven to remain current, continually seeking to augment my music library with fresh material. Staying attuned to new artists and new songs is a delight, providing an open-ended pathway to future enjoyment. This is not a criticism, but rather a personal preference and choice to make the finite infinite.

Of course, this is not to suggest that I am averse to revisiting those glory days through attending performances by the stars of the eighties and nineties. Despite the time-induced graying of the performers and crowd, our recent excursions to see Kansas, Foreigner, and Rob Thomas were great fun.

When visiting with old friends, some of the best times revolve around recounting the good times we had seeing various concerts in the past. Like popcorn bursting in the microwave, we jump from one musical memory to another. Little did we know at the time that those events would be archived in our hearts and minds like treasured photos for a lifetime.

Through time and nonscientific sampling, I have come to realize that my most enjoyable concert experiences have involved seeing Christian music artists. Over the past year, we have been fortunate to see some of our favorite performers—Jesus Culture, Bethel Music, Casting Crowns, Hillsong, Newsboys, MercyMe, and Kari Jobe.

Beyond the undeniable musical talents of each, there are several other elements that make these concerts rise to the top of my figurative charts. The tremendously inspirational content contributes greatly. The atmosphere itself is charged with joy and excitement. Warm exchanges and gestures prevail.

But the single most important differentiator is that all passivity yields to a totally participatory experience. The audience is not simply receiving and enjoying the artists' musical output but instead becomes part of the performance. Giant screens that scroll every lyric from start to finish invite and encourage every person to actively engage in the outpouring of song.

The result is an all-consuming, immersive experience of praise and worship. Joy and thanks fill the air. Looking around and taking it all in, my mind briefly ponders if this might be a little glimpse of heaven.

> **Shout for joy to the Lord, all the earth.**
> **Worship the Lord with gladness; come**
> **before him with joyful songs.**
> **—Psalm 100:1–2 (NIV)**

CHAPTER 6
Bonds of Joy

Morning Coffee, by Gary

Although I have lived in the corporate world for most of my career, my personality tends more toward fluid and flexible than following repeated patterns and rigid schedules. For those of you who have worked for large companies, you know that this goes against the grain of the culture.

Standard practice revolves around regularly scheduled, recurring meetings at set times each month, week, or even day. But because each day brings new circumstances, and surely due to the way that I am wired, avoiding strict regimen and allowing more flexibility to flow with what each day brings has been my preferred approach.

That is all true—except when it comes to morning coffee!

A day without coffee shortly after I rise is like a day without a sunrise. Even on the stormiest day, I think we can all agree that the absence of a sunrise would make for a less than optimal day.

Morning java is not only a pleasure—it is a necessity. The birds don't seem to sing as much without it. The car doesn't seem to stop as quickly on the way to work without it. Solutions and decisions get clouded in your brain. Overall, you are a little slow on the uptake, and your senses are dulled.

Coffee seems to be God's way of easing you into the day, coaxing you out of your REM-induced sluggishness, and sharpening your senses. It is a clear bonus that I crave the taste.

Although it has changed through the years, my current brand of addiction is Dunkin' Donuts original brew—a twenty-four-ounce serving, to be exact. It lasts most of the morning and brings me a measure of pleasure and calm regardless of what challenges are encountered that day.

Some evenings, I even find myself looking forward to the next day's mega cup. That may make it an addiction, but coffee surely makes my list of life's simple pleasures that bring me joy. It provides a little perk to get my day going and a little perk in my step.

Family, by Gary

As these words traverse from my brain to my fingers, I find myself extremely sensitive to the plight of far too many in this world. Family offers a foundation and a great source of joy, but regrettably not everyone is blessed to have the same.

All too often, families are torn apart by divorce, neglect, or death. Children are left to fend for themselves due to abandonment and incarceration.

For those people, the world can be a lonely and intimidating place. My sensitivity derives from the fear of poking a pain point, or even a devastating hurt, by highlighting a blessing enjoyed by many others.

Obviously, I do not want to cause further pain, but that very void for some is the exact reason it is so important for us to truly appreciate the other side. The point is, plain and simple, that having a family is one of the greatest blessings and should never be taken for granted.

Family has often traditionally been defined as immediate in nature—parents and children. It can be more broadly viewed as the extended familial groups of those married couples, including grandparents, aunts, uncles, and cousins. Families can be very large or as small as two.

Regardless of size, the common denominators are love, support, and care.

Strong families provide refuge and comfort. They offer unconditional love. They offer a sympathetic ear or encouragement when things are not going well. They provide dependability and assurance. They offer care and nurturing.

Sadly, for a variety of reasons, not all families check all these boxes. Circumstances can be tough, people are not perfect, but even so, comfort and happiness still may be found.

For those with families that do offer it all, we should be sure to recognize and appreciate how much we are blessed. Part of doing that is cherishing time spent together, as well as showing patience and forgiveness to maintain unity.

Life is short. Life is challenging. Maintaining a close bond with your family makes everything a little bit easier and more joyful.

Regardless of your earthly circumstances, though, we all have an opportunity to be part of a larger, everlasting family—God's family. As much refuge, comfort, and happiness as an earthly family can offer, it pales in comparison to the ultimate joy and peace that comes from our Heavenly Father!

> **How good and pleasant it is when God's people live together in unity!**
> **—Psalm 133:1 (NIV)**

> **A happy family is but an earlier heaven.**
> **—George Bernard Shaw**

Getting Dressed Up, by Tara

We're all familiar with the trope of the little girl trying on Mommy's lipstick and teetering in laughably oversized high heels. She slips on one of her mother's prettiest dresses, dusty pink and so large on a teeny six-year-old's frame that it simply drapes over her shoulders like a tablecloth, the ends trailing on the carpet to her mother's delight. The little girl looks in the mirror, does a twirl or two, and she feels beautiful because she looks like Mommy, and Mommy is beautiful.

Feeling beautiful, just like that little girl, is a wonderful sentiment. Perhaps that little girl was you once upon a time, twirling about in your mother's prettiest dresses. Perhaps you secretly perused your older sister's closet while she was away at school, or maybe you've developed a habit of trying on the eye-catching frocks in window-front displays that you know you won't purchase.

I wouldn't say I'm a "girly girl" to any extreme, and I can't recall playing a whole lot of dress-up as a child, but I *have* always enjoyed getting ready for special events and occasions (prom, winter formals, weddings, and the like). Special occasions that give me an excuse to swipe on a bright red lipstick, spend an hour curling my hair, and twirl about in a swingy dress are such a treat. The prep is truly half the fun of special events, I think. I take it seriously, painstakingly planning out my outfit, hair, and makeup down to nitty-gritty details weeks in advance.

I enjoy dressing up because it gives me an opportunity to feel beautiful. But it's not for myself as much as it is for other people. It's not just about me feeling beautiful in my own eyes, but about feeling beautiful in the eyes of others. If it were all for myself, I would put on makeup, curl my hair, and try on pretty dresses in the privacy of my bedroom every night. But, unfortunately, there's another necessary component: a need to be seen. I feel a need to look good in the eyes of others, to gain approval, or to impress a boy that I like. I feel the need to put on Mommy's heels and lipstick and be told that I look stunning.

We often wag our fingers at this kind of thing, craving attention or seeking happiness through shallow external beauty that will inevitably fade, but I think it's okay to want to dress up and feel beautiful and confident every once in a while. More importantly, I think getting dressed up can serve as a reminder that we may enjoy dressing up physically, but we don't ever have to get dressed up for God.

The truth is, the external stuff doesn't matter. We don't have to try to impress Him because we can't impress Him. He sees our flaws and blemishes clearly underneath the layers of makeup and hairspray. He sees both the good and the bad, and he takes us as we are. Despite our sins, poor judgment calls, and regrettable actions, he sees the beauty inside of each and every one of us, and that's something worth twirling for.

Lifting, by Beth

At the age of sixteen, I started on an unlikely path for a female in the early eighties: I started lifting weights. At that time there were very few women bodybuilders. You rarely saw women in the weight rooms, unless, as athletes, they were sent there by their coaches. It was a time when aerobic conditioning was pursued by ladies as they danced along with Richard Simmons. A few years later, toning and flexibility were the goal with the help of Jane Fonda.

I remember very well my first major purchase toward this new undertaking. It included an adjustable weight bench with a leg-curl attachment and a set of vinyl barbells and dumbbells. A book by Lisa Lyon completed my home gym. The equipment and the book's teaching were a big advancement from the first book I read on this subject, which advised toning up using soup cans and jugs of water. I guess I quickly realized I was going to take this new idea seriously, and I would need to get out of the baby pool rather quickly.

A few things have remained constant in my pursuit of this endeavor from my teenage years until today. The first is location. I started lifting weights in the comfort of my home, and through all these years, I have continued that practice. Currently my husband and I do have a gym membership, but I use it for the tennis privileges and the occasional fitness class, not weight training. My husband has supported my passion for weight training and has blessed me with various pieces of equipment for our home gym, which have met all my workout needs.

I love the freedom that working out by myself, in my own space, provides. I can listen to music at any volume, grimace or grunt all I want without feeling embarrassed, and can run downstairs to move clothes from the washer into the dryer between sets. Of course the short commute is certainly a plus too.

I started on this journey without a tutor and have remained a lone wolf, so to speak, all these years. I became not only a weight lifter but a true student of the sport. I have collected an extensive library of books and magazines to guide me so I could progress in my level of fitness and remain injury free. I also went through training to become a certified personal trainer. I briefly used this certification to train friends and neighbors, but mostly, the additional knowledge was for my own benefit.

I also seek out advice from fellow fitness enthusiasts. In our current home, we live across the street from a former NFL strength and conditioning coach. I would love to download all of his knowledge, but I have to be content with asking for advice only periodically in the hope that I don't become an annoyance to him. Thankfully his wife is a close friend of mine, so he has no choice but to help me. All joking aside, he is always gracious and willing to help anyone in our neighborhood in their pursuit of various fitness goals.

The last constant in my weight lifting career is my continued passion for the sport. I never dread heading into our gym to lift weights. This I cannot say is true when the day's workout plan involves cardio, but that is a story for another time. For me, spending time lifting weights is empowering and fun, challenging yet encouraging. It has been a constant in my life that brings me a sense of stability, and a routine that increases my motivation in all areas of my life. When I finish my workout and exit our home gym, I feel a bit more pep in my step and usually take a can-do attitude with me as I walk down our staircase.

As a teenager I had no way of conceiving how the decision to study this fitness discipline would continue with me throughout my entire life. I could not have known the physical benefits of keeping my muscles strong through decades of life nor of the resulting mental toughness and mood benefits of this practice. Thankfully I was willing to take a step into unknown territory, and the result was many joy-filled hours spent in my home gym.

JOY ALL AROUND US

Cats, by Gary

Truth be told, cats aren't *like* family—they *are* family. For many, it is hard to comprehend our situation when they curiously inquire about it, but it is undeniable on our end.

Not that I haven't desired the cover of plausible deniability many times through the years. You see, it would be much easier to fall within the bounds of man code by attributing our five feline family members to my wife and daughter or some other viable explanation.

My heart and conscience won't allow me to do that, though, as my affection for our cats is second to none. They are undoubtedly a huge part of our household and provide ongoing joy.

Last evening, as we drove home from dinner, Beth briefly bemoaned the full-time job of taking care of our cats. I responded by saying, "They are worth it. What would we do? It would be pretty lonely without them." This immediately drew a smile and complete agreement.

This is not to deny that the cats do require time, attention, effort, nurturing, forgiveness, patience, and love—pretty much the same things that any other family member needs.

Just like any worthwhile investment, though, there is abundant reciprocity. Besides nonstop entertainment, they offer ever-present love and companionship. They defuse frustration, bring calm, and lift your mood.

They are the first to welcome you home. They are also hard to leave as they gaze out the window with a precisely blended combination of sadness and guilt-evoking desperation. Their innate abilities allow them to impart a heavier dose of the latter when they witness the dreaded suitcases in tow.

As any controlling mother-in-law well knows, unspoken words can be the most impactful. Vacations of any length are invariably a little bit less enjoyable, as our lonely, left-behind family members stay in the forefront of our minds. (Until we get online monitoring, we will never know if they are really dancing with lampshades on their heads and swinging from chandeliers in our absence.)

When we do return home after vacation, we find ourselves racing into the house to see them. After the obligatory muted demeanor while greeting us to display their displeasure with being abandoned, our cats quickly snap into a happy and joyful mood. Picture momentary quiet indifference erupting into the Snoopy dance.

As a side note for supporters of The Humane Society, the word *abandoned* here means that a pet sitter visits twice daily to care for our furrier family members, replete with text message updates and action photos.

The fabulous five includes the matriarchal sisters Nike and Puma, whom we adopted as kittens after our cat Prancer passed away when our daughter was six. A couple years later, Beth and Tara rescued the dashing ladies' man Fila from our friends after their cat unexpectedly delivered a litter. He is a real-life version of Tigger and Snagglepuss, all in one.

Next, Adidas grabbed the heart of our daughter on a visit to PetSmart. After abundant pleading and coercing, I found myself driving our family back to the pet superstore just to see her. Needless to say, I had neither the willpower nor the heart to say no, and the expansion moved our status from "weird" to "eccentric."

A year or two later, Reebok showed up on our doorstep and rapidly adopted us. Shortly the diminutive black and white cat permanently moved inside, and my wife quickly nicknamed her *TT*. TT has never articulated what led her to us, but we are pretty confident that word got around the neighborhood about what we affectionately call the Cat Palace, where food, love, and leisure are plentiful.

Sadly, the sweet apple of our daughter's eye, Adidas, suddenly passed away two years ago. This was a blow to all, but my wife was quickly led to a black kitten in a foster home looking for adoption. Pippa was immediately swept into the family and amazingly exhibits striking similarities to Adidas in terms of personality, stature, and mannerisms, right down to her swaying saunter and curled tail tip.

Our family order is as it should be—God, spouse, daughter, and then our five felines. This pecking order does not diminish our cats' collective prominence in our home, though. Without a doubt, they bring immeasurable happiness and joy to our household.

Our house would feel a lot less like home without them.

Joy Found in Loss, by Beth

It is perhaps surprising to say that joy can be found during times of grieving a lost loved one. To admit that joy can coexist with grief seems disrespectful to the person who has passed away. In the bad theology of our minds, we think to ourselves that they might feel unloved if we are joyful now. We know deep in our heart that our lost loved one does not want us to be sad but only wants the best for us, and this includes finding joy within the sorrow.

At this point in my life, having lost both of my parents, I know for certain that joy can spring up unexpectedly during the deeply sad periods of loss and mourning. Interestingly, this joy is not just found as we review photo albums and share happy memories with our family and friends, although walking down memory lane is certainly a good place to put oneself during this time, as it will most definitely provide doses of joy. Memories have a way of strengthening us and solidifying the bonds we had with our lost loved ones, which will help carry us through the healing process we are facing.

My experience has shown me that joy is found most often within the bonds of those still here who are walking with us through the grieving process. In most cases those individuals are family members and intimate friends. Perhaps it is God highlighting to us what blessings still surround us or providing us with a sweet release from the grip of sadness that sometimes feels suffocating and unbearable.

My father passed away before my mother. He was healthy and strong, and he was planning his ninetieth birthday party when a digestive issue took him from us unexpectedly and quickly. The night after his funeral, my mother experienced symptoms that prompted my sister and me to take her to the emergency room. At one point soon after we arrived, I remember thinking *we just buried our father, surely we are not going to lose our mother today!* As we sat in the ER waiting on doctors and tests, the events of the day flashing vividly within our minds, we were certainly not expecting to find joy.

Somehow in those hours spent in the ER, pockets of joy were dropped on us as uncontainable laughter erupted from both my sister and me. If I am remembering correctly, even my mom joined in a few times. I'm sure our lack of sleep from the previous week was partly to blame, but for some unknown reason, we were seeing humor in way too many things. If you are old enough to remember The Mary Tyler Moore Show, think of the "Chuckles the Clown" episode. Thankfully my mother was released that night, and our laughter helped us endure those worry-filled hours.

Family members draw closer together during great periods of loss, highlighting to our conscious minds how grateful we are to have one another. Reflecting on our shared lives and special memories exposes the pervasive joy that family provides at its best. Not all families learn to do life well together, but when they do, it is a powerful force that is always accompanied by joy. I am so grateful to have three siblings to be sharing my life with—all older, I might add (typing that last sentence with an impish grin that usually only the baby in the family masters).

My oldest sister, Debbie, is a teacher at heart; her joy for many years was found in a classroom. She is now retired, but still, in some small way, her teaching gift makes an appearance in most of her conversations. My brother, Richard, is a people person, but not admittedly. He would say his joy is often found in music and playing the drums; I think he finds joy when surrounded by people. My sister Amy is a gentle soul; she often experiences joy through her animals. I believe that laughter is one of her greatest gateways to joy. All of us in various ways reflect the heritage created by our parents. We are a product of their genes, as well as their lifestyle, their beliefs, and their life choices. Although we are now independent and well into creating our own individual family legacies, we are still intricately bonded with one another. This bond, sadly best seen during periods of crisis or mourning, is one of the greatest sources of comfort, security, and joy that family was created to provide.

> **How good and pleasant it is when God's people live together in unity!**
> **—PSALM 133:1 (NIV)**

Date Night with Your Daughter, by Gary

No matter her age, having a date night with your daughter is always a special occasion.

The circumstances of our lives over the past year led to a relative abundance for my daughter and me. When Tara graduated from college, she landed a job that took her to Atlanta. Perhaps not coincidentally, a few months later, I found myself working in Atlanta.

While waiting for our house to sell so we could relocate, I traveled to Atlanta each week, residing in an apartment that was fifteen to thirty minutes away from Tara, traffic willing. Like any outgoing, ambitious college grad, she had lots going on, but we still found time for date nights.

Living in two places and being away from home surely had its pitfalls. Having the opportunity to get together with Tara on a regular basis, though, was a great blessing and source of joy.

Although date night is now frequently dinner accompanied by a glass of wine, in many ways it was not all that different from our earlier "dating career." In essence, it was the same—finding an enjoyable venue to hang out and converse one on one.

Our first such occasion was when Tara was around four or five. One Friday night, my wife had an event with some girlfriends, so this opened the door for a father-daughter date night.

I can still envision the night in my mind's eye. Tara and I both dressed up and headed to Bertucci's, our favorite Italian restaurant. Besides having a station for aspiring pizza chefs to knead and toss dough, they had the second-best pizza on the planet. (Please see my separate essay entitled *Pizza* to reveal the best.)

On this inaugural occasion, there was a little more formality in the air. Tara waited patiently while I opened doors and held the chair out for her, politely thanking me each time. We ended up sitting on the same side of the table, as it seemed more intimate.

The onus was on me to keep conversation rolling that first date. Subsequent dates have become more of a two-way street. Regardless, our first date was very special, just like they continue to be.

> **A wise child brings joy to a father.**
> **—Proverbs 10:1 (NLT)**

Guy Trips, by Gary

Somewhere embedded in the DNA of most men is an innate desire to spend time hanging out with the guys. Regular, bite-sized examples of this include participating in or watching sports together. Whether it's attending a sporting event, playing tennis with three buddies, or simply congregating in front of a TV, each offers a conduit for male bonding.

Occasionally, men have the good fortune to go on what is affectionately known as a "guy trip." Like their more common brethren mentioned above, these trips usually have some type of focal point such as a football game, golf, or an auto race. What differentiates them is duration, distance, and the opportunity to cram in a host of other guy stuff.

At their most fundamental level, guy trips entail group dynamics with lots of testosterone. That typically translates into checking any reasonable semblance of civility at the door, as well as lots and lots of competition. Ping-Pong, poker, darts, pool, volleyball, water polo, horseshoes, cornhole, shuffle alley—and whatever other competition semicreative male minds can conjure up—abound. If someone can find a repetitive activity requiring hand-eye coordination or athleticism that produces winners and losers, sign them up.

Guy trips typically entail copious laughter, sometimes at your own expense. Some of the fun is in the moment; while other fun is recycled by rehashing stories of previous trips. In fact, this in itself can invoke competition as each person searches for the next witty comment or funny anecdote while sitting around the fire pit at 2:00 a.m., as if the Dos Equis guy may show up to recognize the real "Most Interesting Man in the World."

Perhaps as written in man law, every guy trip possesses one unwavering common denominator. Each excursion features massive gastric consumption of mind-blowing proportions—both in terms of quantity and quality. Throwing together the meat lover's grand-slam breakfast with all-day snacking, followed by a massive prime-rib-and-loaded-baked-potato dinner, and then more junk food until you finally turn in is highly inadvisable—especially when the next day mirrors those shampoo directions that counterintuitively instruct, "Rinse and repeat."

A desire to maximize the experience and intrinsic peer pressure couple together to demand that these manly excursions feature late nights. This, in turn, creates a sleep deprivation multiplier effect when combined with extreme indigestion and the inescapable discomfort of sleeping in close quarters with one or more other guys. Besides the restlessness derived from others encroaching on your personal space, deep sleep presents the inherent risk of waking up in the morning with a Sharpie mustache.

Despite the perils and pitfalls, you would be hard-pressed to find a guy who doesn't like guy trips. They are fun. I have great memories of road trips that centered on Philadelphia Eagles games, watching tennis at the US Open, competing in softball tournaments, playing tennis, or just hanging out at the lake.

There is definitely a tipping point, though, when the tsunami of testosterone, stomachaches, and constant companionship starts to kick in. Usually, by the end of the trip, everyone is totally dragging, longingly craving a nap on their personally worn-in couch at home. Unfortunately, we quickly realize this is negated by our need to downplay the notion that our trip was spent mindlessly expending energy and burning the candle at both ends when we walk in the door at home.

And to make matters worse, our absence has created both the pent-up demand for and necessary time to formulate an abundant list of joint activities and pressing chores. My keen male instincts inform me that it may land with a thud if I say, "Sorry, honey, you go ahead to do birthday shopping alone because I am totally beat from hanging out with the guys."

Although taking a trip with a bunch of guys has its downside, we happily sign up for the next trip when the opportunity arises. The actual event, not to mention reminiscing about it later, is surely a great time. Perhaps the greatest joy, though, is settling back in at home.

Band Encore, by Gary

Simply attending a concert makes you pretty happy. This is particularly true if you see one of your favorite bands or singers. Usually by design, the excitement and enjoyment build, culminating with the encore.

Also by design, bands hold out one of their most popular and best songs for the encore. No matter how good the music to that point, there usually seems to be a little bit of a noticeable void. Anticipation builds for that one missing hit.

The encore serves as the climax after the band somewhat cruelly feigns that they have concluded for the evening. The band ritualistically leaves the stage, but the lights remain low, signaling that there is still reason for hope. The crowd waves lit cell phones, claps, and screams to coax the band to return—the old-schoolers even hoist flaming lighters in the air.

Most bands tend to reward the audience by performing two songs for their encore, only to depart the next time for good.

Some bands elevate the joyousness further by throwing in a second curtain call. At that point, you know the band will either leave you still wanting with a great song unplayed or emerge once again to finish off the concert on an even higher note.

It usually doesn't get much better than that. You exit the concert still pumped up, knowing you have witnessed one for the ages.

After any encore, the crowd tends to linger a little bit, wanting more and needing evidence that the concert is truly over. Once the lights come up and the roadies make their way out on stage to start tearing things down, it is finally safe to make your way to the exits.

Seeing a favorite performer in concert is great. One encore or two—ending on a high is even better!

CHAPTER 7
Kindness and Joy

The Joy of Children, by Beth

Yesterday at church, I received a hug from a sweet eight-year-old girl named Ella. As I have only recently gotten to know her and was caught up in other things when it happened, the hug came as a total surprise. Needless to say, it melted my heart. Joy quickly arises in me when children are around. It doesn't matter if I know them or I am just a quiet observer of their antics from across a store or restaurant. For me, it occurs whether I see precious newborns, busy toddlers, curious preschoolers, energetic grade-schoolers, or independent adolescents. I can appreciate the uniqueness that each life stage brings and very much enjoy watching individual life stories unfold.

Children of all ages remind us of the many possibilities of life. We can see the world with a pure lens when we explore things with the help of those who are younger and have been less shaped and limited in their thinking by the world. Children exhibit freedom in their lives at a level that is totally foreign to most adults.

Running around a room singing and dancing, just because, is the norm for children. Creating things from anything and everything that is in front of them is as well. We might watch a five-year-old create a picture from the unwanted food on his dinner plate as he silently hopes he won't have to stay in his seat much longer. Blankets become forts, or capes; kitchen pan lids become cymbals; paper towel rolls become telescopes. Literally the sky is the limit when you have a child's imagination. The world around them is theirs for the taking, and they use their resources well!

Children's thoughts are most always uncensored as well. Listening to the musings and questions of two-year-olds to thirteen-year-olds and beyond certainly supplies shots of joy. Often the seriousness of their processing or questions prevents us from responding out loud in the form of laughter. We silently nod and allow them to continue as we make a mental note to record this most recent gem in our journal.

Children usually put no limits on who they can be both in the present and in the future. They draw on their imaginations and props at hand to become firefighters, doctors, princesses, and dragons. When children are asked to share what they want to be when they grow up, the answer usually changes depending on the day, but it never has fear or doubt attached to it. From president to actress to astronaut to brain surgeon, all are believed to be available for the taking.

As I reflect on characteristics of children, it is not surprising they are joyful. Their inherent tendencies both promote joy and insulate them from sadness. Perhaps in our path to adulthood we have laid aside ways of thinking and experiencing life that would benefit us to pick back up. I am thankful for the sweet reminders of how life can be better experienced from the ways of those much younger than me. I will welcome both their joy and their hugs anytime they are offered.

> **Children are a gift from the Lord; they are a reward from him. Children born to a young man are like arrows in a warrior's hands. How joyful is the man whose quiver is full of them!**
> **—Psalm 127:3-5 (NLT)**

Naps, by Gary

Many times, you do not need to give it much thought—your body takes over, and a short while later, you are scrambling to see how much time has passed. Naps just sort of happen when the circumstances are right—although, if you are like me, timing isn't always opportune.

Most can probably relate to falling asleep in a movie, which can be mildly embarrassing. Comparatively, though, this is way better than nodding off in the second pew or your high school history class. As unfortunate as those may be, I have seen and experienced worse.

For instance, there was the time that several of us debated whether the high-priced consultant in the conference room was "dead to the world." Our collective narcoleptic sensory skills resoundingly agreed that his heavy breathing and the slight intermittent buzz on his lips were all the evidence we needed.

Several years ago, while I was working at a large corporation, whispers persisted that a recently hired top executive had a tendency to fall asleep in meetings. I am sure executive coaches and human resource experts would all agree that this can be somewhat of a career-limiting move. It is unclear whether there was a connection, but it is worth noting that this executive had a very short tenure with the company.

As I think about it, the skills necessary to fall asleep anytime, anyplace—or the skills not to—are not typically listed on resumes or discussed in an interview. Fortunately—not that I haven't longed for a nap some days at the office—my internal body clock and caffeinated beverage intake have circumvented those occurrences thus far.

This does not mean that I have been totally immune to inopportune snoozing. A few years ago, we were heading to the airport to return home after visiting family in Pennsylvania for Christmas. During our visit, I contracted a severe case of the flu. Considering that our plane was still on schedule and a snowstorm had descended on the area, I decided it would be best for me to take the wheel. Midway to the airport, my wife and daughter were dismayed to discover that I had dozed off while waiting at what must have been an interminably long red light.

Fortunately, most naps do not come with a backstory and do provide a much-needed boost. A quick snooze before heading out for a late evening can mean the difference between stumbling through the motions and having a good time. A refreshing nap can transform exhausted, irritable, and cranky into perky, engaged, and congenial.

Naps can also provide a brief period of escape from the challenges of the world around us. It's a little bit like being an ostrich, but with your head on a pillow or back rest.

My personal favorite is the fifteen-minute power nap. Somehow this brief shutdown provides the antidote when you are dragging from a late night, an overly ambitious schedule, heavy physical activity, or stressful circumstances. A quick respite recharges your batteries so you can take on the rest of the day with a smile.

On the weekends, mixing in a nap on a lazy afternoon can provide a contented, joyful feeling. There is something very liberating and satisfying in stealing a little time for yourself and pushing aside the abundant chores waiting on your mental to-do list. And the colder or wetter the day, the better.

Perhaps naps fall short of joy on the emotional scale, but they at least offer a shot of comfort and happiness. Even if the nap itself doesn't produce joy, the renewed energy that results from a short snooze surely helps make other activities joyful.

Simple Rituals, by Beth

Unlike both of my cowriters in this endeavor, I am not a coffee lover. I don't remember even once having the desire to start the habit of drinking coffee. The few times that I have tasted it confirmed to me that my lack of desire was for very good reason. Coffee enthusiasts, and from my experience this seems to include everyone except me, apparently love the taste. I'm sure the extra energy supplied by the caffeine is part of the appeal of coffee as well. Taste and caffeine addiction aside, I think there is another aspect of coffee consumption that endears its faithful enthusiasts to return to it daily, if not multiple times each day.

The additional attraction to coffee, I believe, is the joy and comfort of the daily ritual or routine that drinking it revolves around.

Your coffee ritual might start with a good-bye kiss as your spouse hands you a warm thermos cup and you head out for the day. Fighting through the morning traffic and contemplating the day ahead, you find some calm as you savor the warm beverage made for you with love.

Perhaps you drink it alone at home as you read the morning paper. You may also be considering what the day before you holds, but you are more concerned about staying up to date with what is happening in your local community and beyond. Maybe without you even realizing it, the routine and sameness provided by your coffee-filled mug are somewhat of an anchor in the chaotic world so often detailed in the ink of our daily newsprint.

I imagine with the proliferation of coffee houses around our country, many of you have a favorite place you frequent daily where you can get your java made precisely to your liking and the baristas know you by name. As the theme song from *Cheers* reminded us years ago, there truly is comfort, and dare I say joy, in being somewhere where everyone knows your name.

Nothing similar to these daily routines was a part of my life until a few months ago. A good friend of mine who was following a new health and diet plan mentioned that part of it involved drinking hot water with lemon before breakfast. I had heard about the many benefits of this practice, so I decided I would try it out and see what, if any, benefits I might realize.

What I found was not a typical health benefit per se. Instead the benefit was on a more personal and even spiritual level. My morning now has a ritual that involves a hot beverage, and it has become almost nonnegotiable.

I don't walk into a coffee house and order a drink to my specifications, but instead I remove one of my favorite mugs from our cabinet and add water. I heat the water for exactly ninety seconds in our microwave and then heat a lemon for fifteen. After I squeeze the lemon juice in the water, my drink is ready. Made to order, with my specifications, by me. Somewhere nearby is my husband (unless he is out on his morning coffee run to Dunkin' Donuts), who always knows my name.

I don't enjoy my beverage as I fight my way through morning traffic, but it still provides a calm to the start of my day and is a welcome addition as I sit at our kitchen table or, weather permitting, cozy up on the couch that resides on our back porch. Both of these locations allow me to enjoy the view of our backyard, complete with birds, squirrels, and the traffic of a nearby road.

I don't normally add reading the newspaper to my early-morning ritual but instead grab our varied stack of devotion-filled books that my husband and I share. Like a newspaper, my daily reading choice is referenced by date. Unlike the words often on newsprint, however, my reading material is always uplifting, always encouraging, and always inspiring. When I finish my daily reading, I know that together with my true anchor, I can face whatever the day throws at me.

In the stillness of the morning, as I watch the steam rising from my mug, mostly I am grateful. Grateful for a host of things, and also for my hot beverage and the joy of simple rituals.

JOY ALL AROUND US

Hanging Around Joyful People, by Gary

Osmosis is a scientific term describing an occurrence of nature. It is a complicated action not easily explained, but in nature it typically refers to one liquid permeating another. It usually happens subtly, without any visible evidence.

Plants absorbing water and minerals is an example of osmosis. Simply by being present around the plant, these elements infiltrate it.

Osmosis occurs in the nonmolecular realms as well. Surrounding yourself with negative people tends to evoke negative thinking. Conversely, happy individuals with perpetual smiles and quick laughter tend to draw the same from others around them over time.

In sports, team chemistry can make the difference between winning and losing. Adding players with a winning attitude and history of success can suddenly transform a moribund team prone to failure. It may not be tangible, but it is a very real phenomenon. Mixing in some seasoned veterans to lead and mentor a group of talented young upstarts is a proven formula for success.

Joy is often like osmosis—it permeates others in a very subtle, invisible way.

It has become clear to me that hanging around joyful people brings me joy! They view the world through "half-full" lenses, recognizing all the reasons for celebration around them. Just as our mission for this book is to call out many reasons for daily joy, those individuals notice the abundant blessings that might be routinely overlooked.

Joyful people are walking "don't sweat the small stuff" mentors without even knowing it. Little things—even big things—don't get them down or keep them down. Life surely comes with heartaches and challenges, but joyful people rebound quickly.

Joining fifty thousand of your closest friends at one of your favorite team's big games is a great way to rub elbows with joyful people—at least as long as events are going your way. All is fun and games until the other team prevails. The mood shifts abruptly when your team lands on the losing side of the ledger. This type of joy is conditional and can be very fleeting, particularly if your team is not a juggernaut.

My favorite place to surround myself with joyful people is church. Here you find brothers and sisters with an undeniable grounding and inner peace. There is nothing like the joy of the Lord residing within you—it sustains itself and is not conditional.

The more I am around my fellow church members, the more I want to be around them. They radiate warmth and happiness with their smiles, gestures, kind words, and gentle touch. Their joy is infectious, imperceptibly permeating others around them.

Those osmotic recipients, in turn, infect others. Of course, this wonderful phenomenon is not confined to a church setting—it follows them wherever they go. Every interaction, smile, and gesture offers an opportunity to spread a little bit of happiness, if not joy.

If you are looking for joy, start hanging out with joyful people. There is surely something to the company you keep. After some time, you may even notice that others are seeking to hang out with you!

> **May the God of hope fill you with all joy and peace as you trust in him, so that you may overflow with hope by the power of the Holy Spirit.**
> **—Romans 15:13 (NIV)**

A Childlike Sense of Wonder and Excitement, by Tara

Take a moment to remember what it's like to look at life through the lens of a child. Everything is fresh and exciting, because everything is new. It doesn't take much to impress or excite a young child, because their eyes and ears are so young and their experiences so limited.

When I was a child, I loved revolving doors. The first time I entered a revolving door, I found it astounding. I wanted to keep running through it, pushing the door round and round in circles. I wanted to exit and enter, and exit and enter again. It was this new, exciting thing that I had never seen before—who could blame me?

Today, I've seen my fair share of revolving doors, and the thrill of using one has since died. Not only has the thrill died, but I don't even particularly like them anymore. I fear someone in another compartment pushing the door faster than I can walk, thus shoving me in the ankles, yet I also find that the doors are often too heavy for me to quickly gain momentum alone.

I understand the functionality of revolving doors, the energy-saving purpose of them, but I avoid them when given the option. At my office building, there is a revolving door and regular push/pull doors on either side. The regular doors feature a lovely sign asking users to "please use the revolving door." I almost always disobey the sign and tug open the regular door, swiftly moving past those who remain trapped in the glass merry-go-round.

I think this is fairly common. Not the abstinence from revolving doors, but the deterioration of our sense of childlike wonder. We grow older, our experiences multiply, and things that were once thrilling become common and mundane. We become difficult to impress. We're no longer children; we're adults with "seen it all before" attitudes.

It's easy to fall into this frame of mind and forget to take note of the everyday splendors around us, but I think it can behoove each and every one of us to look at life through the lens of a child every now and then.

I've found that I can tap into this childlike sense of wonder when I visit aquariums. I become transfixed by the rhythmic and deft swish of a shark's tail and am left in awe by the harlequin tropical rainbow fish.

It's an especially wonderful treat when an aquarium offers a shallow stingray pool in which visitors can interact with the fish. The stingrays seem to wear perpetual smiles, and they love to dazzle onlookers by jumping toward outstretched hands and creating a splash. I find myself giddy in these moments, as if nothing else matters. I find myself with a widespread smile, just like a child.

I think that's important. Growing up and maturing are important, but don't ever totally let go of your sense of childlike wonder.

What's your revolving door? What have you become desensitized to? What childlike thrill has died?

More importantly, what's your aquarium? I encourage you to find it and hold on to it. Hold on to your aquarium tightly.

Outdoor Dining, by Gary

"In or out?" That is often the last-second question from my wife before I drop her off at the door of a restaurant. That split-second decision might define the entire experience.

There are myriad considerations in making this decision. Some of the key factors might include the temperature, the likelihood of rain, wind speeds, humidity levels, the ambience of the outdoor setting, shade or sun availability, entertainment options, chair comfort, our chosen attire, table availability, and effectiveness of the interior ventilation system. (We both hate leaving the restaurant smelling like we just seared sundry meats on the grill and deep-fried some jumbo onion rings.)

I am sure that I am missing a factor or two, but you get the idea. Although there might be many reasons to sit inside, Beth and I both share a bias toward dining outside. And despite my temperature window tending to be a bit wider than her comfort range, especially on the cool side, we are on the same page 90 percent of the time.

Insects and weather permitting, the bottom line is that we both experience added enjoyment dining outside.

There is something peaceful and pleasing about simply taking in the splendor of a nice day. Combining this with some delicious food, prepared by someone else while you comfortably relax, only adds to the sentiment.

The happiness quotient ascends further from there if there is also a local artist strumming the guitar and singing familiar tunes, interesting pedestrians strolling by, striking nature or wildlife, or simply a body of water with all its related accompaniments within sight.

It is worth noting, too, that compensating factors come into play here. For instance, a beautiful day or football on the large-screen TV can overcome a parking-lot view. Or a nearby dock or waterfall might make up for cushionless wrought-iron chairs or a table needing a half dozen sugar packs to balance.

Outdoors, the pace gets a little slower as you take in everything around you, soaking in the natural light or gazing at the gently sparkling stars. The conversation seems to be a little more leisurely and stimulating. The slight breeze intermittently cools you on a warm day, and the rays of sun warm you on a cooler day.

Much like when you grab a window table on the thirty-first floor downtown, the food quality often gets graded on a curve the better the outdoor setting. Our perception of the food quality tends to align with the perception of everything else around us. What a joy when good food and a great outdoor setting come together.

> **So go ahead. Eat your food with joy, and drink your wine with a happy heart, for God approves of this!**
> **—Ecclesiastes 9:7 (NLT)**

Intentional Acts of Kindness, by Gary

Kindness describes the heart of the individual who is initiating benevolence. The impact is intended for the recipient, but acts of kindness have a way of imparting joy on both parties.

The phrase "random acts of kindness" describes a recipient's perspective when the benevolence is unexpected. Sometimes kind acts seemingly emerge out of the blue like a lightning bolt of goodness. Of course, a congenial nature might form a figurative lightning rod to attract these high-voltage bolts. You tend to reap what you sow.

I can also attest that sometimes the opposite is true. Several months ago on my habitual morning coffee run before heading to the office, stress rose within me as the clock ticked toward an early meeting start time. The drive-through line was moving painfully slowly, and I grumbled to myself when the car in front of me continued to sit at the menu board rather than move up to the window. The driver eventually regained focus and proceeded forward. With an eye on the clock, and still a bit annoyed as I pulled up to the window, the words did not immediately register when the barista informed me there was no charge. Perhaps the driver ahead saw my frustration in his rearview mirror, simply wanted to do something nice, or routinely commits acts of kindness—but he picked up my tab.

His kind act immediately transformed my mood. My annoyance lifted. Happiness invaded. And perhaps more importantly, humbleness set in. His gesture surely wasn't warranted by my behavior, but it did stir a change in me from that day forward. Fighting through traffic in rush hour has always evoked the worst in me, regardless of whether it was contained to self-talk. Although sometimes I feel the old muscle memory starting to kick in as I navigate the traffic turmoil, impatience and annoyance have been almost solely replaced with calm and grace.

Although he did not witness my reaction, the gentleman likely drove away from the coffee shop that day with at least a little sense of joy. Simply put, it feels good to do nice things for others. And my suspicion is that he knew the ripple effect would positively touch others that day.

This leads me to an important point. His benevolence might have been a gut reaction to seeing my furrowed brow, but it was deliberate. Random acts of kindness require intentional acts of kindness on the flip side.

Living our lives with intentional kindness surely imparts joy to others—and invokes joy within ourselves.

This is a life choice that pays dividends. Happiness and joy are subconsciously contagious, but we can consciously choose to carry the contagions.

Reflect on how you feel when you tip generously to reward attentive service or a particularly engaging server at a restaurant. Or when you converse with them in a friendly manner and express thanks for their efforts. It makes you feel good to know that the other person feels appreciated, not to mention delighted by some extra cash. It's funny, too, how the next time you meet up with that server, you feel a little like old friends.

Receiving random acts of kindness is always a great thing. Committing intentional acts of kindness is even better—all the way around.

> **But the fruit of the Spirit is love, joy, peace, forbearance, kindness, goodness, faithfulness, gentleness and self-control.**
> **—Galatians 5:22-23 (NIV)**

Life's Little Luxuries, by Gary

Firmly planted in the new millennium, we have become accustomed to a growing number of conveniences. Some of these are major changes from the past, while others are relatively minor and often easily overlooked.

The Internet, along with advances in computer and mobile technology, has fueled many of the major enhancements. Enterprising and progressive manufacturers, vendors, and service providers increasingly find ways to embrace technology to simplify our lives or offer differentiating value-added features and services.

Although Black Friday proves that physical shopping hasn't yet gone the way of the dinosaur, online shopping has increasingly provided a more convenient and time-effective alternative. With a few clicks, you can find exactly what you want—any day, any time, and without braving the elements.

It should be noted, though, that for those who prefer the whole experience of bouncing from store to store in search of the perfect gift or outfit—the opportunity remains. You can still have your cake and eat it too—and with a little less of a crowd.

The conveniences extend way beyond shopping, though, as we can communicate with our doctors through secure portals, get prescriptions filled electronically, register for classes, view movies, arrange food delivery, remotely control our thermostat, play DJ on our sound system, and perform seemingly endless other tasks from our laps or the palms of our hands. We can adjust our house lights, enable or disable our alarm system, or watch what is happening inside our home anywhere on the planet with Internet or cellular connection.

These methods are quickly becoming commonplace or even the norm, so it stands to reason that the convenience is easily overlooked. If not an outright convenience, it surely is at least a bit of addition by subtraction. By eliminating inconveniences, we gain the highly precious commodity of time and perhaps avoid a withdrawal from our "joy account."

While driving earlier today, I passed a man mowing his lawn. No one has figured out how to groom the grass digitally just yet, but autopilot lawn care is a luxury that I enjoy. The homeowners' associations of our two most recent homes have taken care of the entire neighborhood's lawn care. This not only means that everyone's yard is nicely groomed, but I never have to even start up a mower or whack some weeds.

This has become my new normal, which I quite frankly take for granted. How many other little luxuries do we all tend to forget?

CHAPTER 8
'Tis the Season of Joy

Bonds of Love, by Gary

Shortly after one of our cats showed up on our doorstep and adopted us, she and I developed an extraordinary bond. She typically likes to be near me—or more specifically, on me—when I am home.

When I am working at my desk, the pacing back and forth in front of the computer monitor is a bit of a challenge. Reebok (or TT, as my wife affectionately nicknamed the diminutive cat) clearly wants a little more attention than what I have to offer, and she can be remarkably persistent. This battle of wills typically ends with her on my lap while I do my best Stretch Armstrong imitation with the keyboard, or she hunkers down to sun herself under one of my desk lamps.

Sitting down to watch TV or read a book usually precipitates a jump into my lap for a little catnap or to watch the world go by. Even if she is nowhere in sight when I take a seat, Reebok's extraordinary extrasensory cat powers somehow have her coiled at my feet within seconds.

Now, let me make something clear here. Some may see this as an annoyance, but that couldn't be further from the truth for me. This companionship makes me very happy, whether I am working, relaxing, or retiring for the evening.

And speaking of nighttime routine, there is definitely a routine. When I settle in to sleep (or for some late-night TV viewing, which inevitably leads to drifting off into nocturnal bliss), TT begins her evening protocol. She begins with about a twenty-minute bonding session on my chest, marked by the rumblings of a gentle, persistent purr. Next, she heads south and nests on my legs, rolling into a cat ball to collect some z's.

Throughout the night, as long as my movements are not too radical, she adjusts to the changing landscape, peacefully sleeping on or beside me until it is time to rise. Occasionally, some other sibling cat antics in the middle of the night or an emerging fur ball might interfere with this regimen, but most nights you can book it.

It's a special privilege to have your advocate always with you. I wouldn't want it any other way.

JOY ALL AROUND US

September Magazines, by Beth

My love for magazines started at a young age, first with *Archie* comic books purchased from our local ice cream shop, later with *Young Miss* and *Teen* magazines delivered directly to our mailbox. The September issues of these teen fashion magazines quickly became my favorite of the year. I can still remember the joy and excitement I felt when the coveted issue would arrive on a hot August day. It would be read multiple times, taken with me to our local pool to share with friends, and then retired to a bedroom shelf.

Here, within the glossy pages, I would find advice on the best back-to-school fashions and learn new ways to style my hair and ten ways to make this my best school year ever! What more could a teenage girl want, other than the interest of her latest crush? As I remember, there was no shortage of advice on that topic either.

As time went on, the September issues got thicker and thicker. I didn't care that most of the content was advertisements. I loved the ads as well. These advertisements taught me about the best shampoo and mascara, how to eliminate acne, and what toothpaste would make my breath kissable. As I was a less discerning consumer at the time, an ad in *Teen* magazine was enough of an endorsement for me.

Today still, for no logical reason, my heart races to see the September issues of fashion magazines on display at the grocery store checkouts. The September issues I now read, although not geared to the back-to-school crowd, are still the thickest issues of the year. And I still get excited, and a bit nostalgic, as I open the cover to discover the secrets waiting inside.

Baseball Stadiums, by Gary

We all have special places or situations that provide a particular visceral lift. For some, it might be visiting a childhood vacation spot, running a race, getting ice cream at the parlor you frequented as a kid, or the anticipation of Christmas.

For me, visiting my favorite baseball stadium elicits a special feeling and great memories. My pulse quickens a little when my eyes first gaze at the field as a rush of nostalgia and comfort courses through my body. Apparently, I am not the only one, as the movie *Field of Dreams* seemed to tap into those same emotions for a large number of people.

Having also spent a great deal of time competing between the white lines myself, some of these good feelings derive from those days of conquest. It extends much beyond that, though, as my senses take in everything from the smell of the fresh-cut grass to the crack of the bat as players pound balls into the stands during batting practice to the perfectly manicured field to the other smiling fans similarly observing around me.

On particularly introspective days, my mind takes me on a whirlwind tour down memory lane. I fondly recall coaxing my father out to play catch or Wiffle ball in the backyard early in my budding baseball career. I remember my first Little League opening day ceremony and my first college baseball game. I recall the first time I stepped into a baseball stadium to watch the players I had only seen on baseball cards and TV.

From those early days to even now, I marvel at the grand design and construct of these monolithic stadiums. Baseball is not a cookie-cutter sport and the venues tend to reflect this with their varied dimensions and designs. The lines, materials, and layouts flow almost poetically. Creativity is abundant and the sky is the limit—perhaps unless the design incorporates a dome. During my days of youth, when time seemed more infinite, these athletic battlegrounds inspired me to spend countless hours sketching my own designs. Although I never became the baseball version of Frank Lloyd Wright, the passion still bubbles within me.

For what it is worth, the stadium that is particularly magical to me is Citizens Bank Park in Philadelphia. Although it is approaching twenty years that we have lived in the South, my childhood-hometown Phillies are still in my heart. The park itself is a tremendous blend of old-time nostalgia and modern-day convenience that opens in center field to a skyline view of the city. Despite the baseball diamond being quite expansive, the ballpark exudes an intimate feel with seats and sight lines drawn close to the field.

Citizens Bank Park is one of the many modern-retro stadiums that have been constructed over the past couple decades, spawned by the enormous success and popularity of Baltimore's Camden Yards. And, beyond the architectural and atmospheric charm itself, the baseball park renaissance elevated another major source of joy to a higher level—great food! Although the truth still remains that hot dogs just taste a little better at the ballpark, the new designs added-in quality restaurants, open-air sports bars overlooking the field, and locally popular food vendors. While Dempsey's crab cakes and Boog's BBQ are staples at Camden Yards, Tony Luke's cheesesteaks, Chickie and Pete's crab fries, and Bull's BBQ are huge favorites at Citizens Bank Park.

As a little bit of an aside, I received an unexpected and incredible blessing a couple years ago when I took a new position. My office overlooked the left-field wall of a new minor league stadium constructed as a replica of Fenway Park in Boston. For the first couple months, I had to pinch myself as I walked past the stadium's main gate on my way to the office, and I felt a twisted pleasure at hearing baseballs thud off the windows during batting practice.

As you can tell, I much prefer to arrive to the ballpark early and take everything in before the game actually commences. It never bores me and simply makes me feel a real sense of joy. The game itself is a bonus.

Christmas, by Gary

The seasons of our lives have brought different circumstances, activities, and traditions surrounding Christmas, but an unwavering constant throughout the years has been the presence of joy. What an awesome way to close out each year that is wrought with its own earthly toil and challenges.

Celebrating the birth of Jesus instills a heavenly calm in the air and an extra measure of peace in our hearts. Cheerful, melodic, and comforting Christmas songs fill the air, wallpapering the holiday season with happiness and joy. No matter the changing locations and circumstances, the Christmas spirit prevails.

When I was growing up, Christmastime brought advent calendars to count down the days, driving around town on snow-dusted roads to admire holiday lighting displays, and thoughtfully creating wish lists. My youngest days included expectantly watching for Santa Claus to roll into town on a fire truck Thanksgiving night, followed by a fleeting, unnerved-by-the-gravity-of-the-moment visit to his quaint, red-shingled house located outside the local pharmacy—about 3,400 miles south of the North Pole.

It meant baking almost every type of Christmas cookie imaginable—Toll House, oatmeal, pinwheels, snickerdoodles, peanut butter, sugar cut-outs, peanut butter cups, snowballs, and other more froufrou varieties—and then packing them away in their own dedicated Christmas tins for daily consumption until the annual New Year's caloric-conscious-ness kicked back in.

It meant making a place for the plywood platform crafted by my father that displayed a snow-covered village with lit buildings and operating miniature trains. It meant wishing for a well-timed snowfall to provide a Hallmark-worthy, picturesque, and peaceful white Christmas Day.

Christmas always involved lots and lots of decorations. Lights trimmed the exterior of the house, while the interior was adorned with collections of angels, Santas, snowmen, Dickens characters, pillows in shades of red and green, holiday throws, and wreaths. Candles were placed inside each window throughout the house, offering a warm, peaceful glow. Festive dishes and glassware came out of storage to replace the more pedestrian, less joyful everyday stuff. Even paintings were switched out to seasonally themed artwork.

Think Griswold with elegance. From Thanksgiving to New Year's Day—our family was clearly all in with the joy of the Christmas season!

The traditions and festivities find their roots in my mother, who continues to be the Chief Correspondent of Christmas Joy. Some of this holiday spirit was planted by my grandparents' gift-giving generosity, but my mother has groomed that seedling into an expansive, fully blooming arbor. The rest of us quickly caught that spirit and have happily joined in.

Annual childhood custom called for a trip to a local farm shortly after Thanksgiving to pick out the perfect fresh-cut Christmas tree, followed by a group effort in decorative collaboration. Beth and I adopted this tradition in our newly formed household for many years until the feline proclivity to briefly consume needles and subsequently deposit them in sundry locations finally persuaded us that an artificial tree might be a better option.

Well stocked with many accumulated Christmas-themed gifts, our home has never lacked for festive décor. Shortly after Thanksgiving, Beth and Tara begin the interior transformation by artfully arranging our own, less extensive collection of holiday decorations.

The season has usually involved dedicating time to help brighten the days of others less fortunate. As a youth, this meant braving the cold and snow to spread a little holiday cheer with our youth group, parking ourselves on various doorsteps singing Christmas carols and then thawing our hands, feet, and noses afterward back at the church and enjoying hot chocolate, cookies, and pent-up energy release.

The Christmas season has meant volunteering time and donating to efforts such as Toys for Tots, Christmas Angels, and Operation Christmas Child. It has also involved buying and delivering gifts and meals to help families in need celebrate Christmas. Although always greatly appreciated by the recipients, it has been my experience that these times of serving have perhaps offered greater joy to those giving than those receiving. It truly is better to give than to receive.

Speaking of gifts, did I mention my enthusiasm for finding the perfect gifts for family and friends? As detailed elsewhere, I truly love giving, but for many years this translated into an obsessive month-long quest. Fortunately, I have learned to strike a balance through the years.

Tara's own little tradition unknowingly and humbly provided some of the most perfect gifts. At an early age, she began crafting special gifts for our extended family. Paper, Popsicle sticks, pom-poms, glitter, glue, markers, paint, photos, clay, and whatever else her creative mind specified were used to make holiday decorations, calendars, greeting cards, T-shirts, coffee table books, and more. Little did she know that these would become some of the most cherished gifts of the season.

The building anticipation of Christmas morning and the surprises that might await has carried through the years, albeit with a shift in point of view. The childhood excitement of receiving gradually transitioned more into the joy of giving. Although we all can fully enjoy Christmas, rejoicing through the unfettered eyes of children is extra special.

For decades, my parents' tradition was to host an open house immediately following our church's Christmas Eve candlelight service. This apparently also became a tradition for many other families in our small town, as the event was pretty much standing room only even on the snowiest days. The fun began as we worked diligently for days preparing a diverse, plentiful spread for this large gathering and then continued as we socialized at the party with an undeniable spirit of joy and anticipation in the air.

The Christmas Eve service itself was always a highlight of the season—perhaps the year. An undeniable feeling of comfort and peace filled the church, lit only with handheld candles as the congregation sang "Joy to the World," "Angels We Have Heard on High," and "Silent Night." Although we left this behind when we moved away, our new church provided its own special moments. One year, a spontaneous standing ovation erupted after the worship team performed a tremendously moving rendition of "My Deliverer." The song created such a buzz that the congregation was treated to an encore performance the following year, once again drawing a standing ovation.

The Christmas season has always been about enjoying time with family and friends. In my youth, grandparents coming to visit or a road trip to see them added to the excitement of the season. Holiday lunches, drop-ins, and parties continue to dot the calendar in the weeks leading up to Christmas.

After we moved to Charlotte when our daughter was five, a new tradition began for our small nuclear family. Leaving both extended families behind in Pennsylvania put planes, trains, automobiles, and sleighs into the holiday mix for us—well, at least it felt like we had every mode of transportation covered. This was not always without adventure when you consider our travel to a northern climate prone to snow and the more contemporary "wintry mix."

Because we wanted to attend our own church's Christmas Eve service and experience Christmas morning at home, the itinerary called for an early rise and then a late-morning break for the airport. Some years flight schedules remained on time, other years not so much. One memorable moment was landing in Philadelphia early, but then waiting ninety minutes for the airport to find someone among its skeleton crew who could operate the Jetway to deplane us. Typically, though, dogged determination allowed us to arrive at my parents' home in time for the plentiful feast lovingly prepared by my mother—eighteen inches of fresh-fallen snow or not.

As most married couples know, coordinating activities on both sides of the family is not always easy. We have been fortunate that Beth's family tradition has been to gather the day after Christmas, enabling us to spend time and celebrate with everyone. Many years, we have also been fortunate to work in celebration with our closest friends on Christmas Eve before embarking on our Christmas Day journey, spreading out the Christmas Day celebration to a full three days.

Over the past few years, we have pushed up the trek north to the night before Christmas, which makes for a less frantic and more peaceful Christmas Day. It has also put us around the table for a decadent Christmas-morning brunch rather than a quick bite of fresh-baked buns and a sprint to catch a flight—adding more culinary delight to the day, along with some girth to our waistlines.

For our family, like many others, the period from Thanksgiving to New Year's is a time to rejoice and recharge. It is a time to reflect on our blessings and draw closer to our family and friends. It is a time to show our love and appreciation to others.

Joy is widely associated with Christmas, particularly considering it is the ultimate source of this euphoric state. Our family has clearly fully embraced it, celebrating this most sacred and world-altering day with abundance. My parents instilled the joy of the Christmas season into our family from our earliest memories. And although we rejoice on this important day and throughout the holiday season each year, the reason for celebration offers a joy that endures for eternity.

> **When they saw the star, they were filled with joy!**
> **—Matthew 2:10 (NLT)**

> **Christmas is joy, religious joy, an inner joy of light and peace.**
> **—Pope Francis**

Listening to Music with Headphones, by Gary

There is nothing like throwing on some headphones and listening to music. For me, the experience is further intensified in the dark.

The music envelops me. The lyrics are sharpened. Emotions are tapped and triggered. Time slows down.

Somehow, listening to music with headphones seemingly allows me to get inside my own head. Who needs to hire a shrink when a pair of Beats or Bose will suffice?

Sometimes the headphones allow me to simply rock out listening to heavy power chords, soaring vocals, and high-energy music. Other times the headphones allow me to contemplate every word and reflect on life. Sometimes the headphones allow me to shut out the world and commune with God.

There is no doubt—music brings me joy. If I can't be live and in person witnessing my favorite recording artists up close and personal, my next choice is to wrap myself in the musical cocoon offered by my headphones.

I do some of my best thinking in that cocoon, possibly only rivaled by the shower, middle-of-the-night awakenings, cross-country flights, and driving on a dark, desolate highway.

Listening to music through headphones also might be the best alternative to Ambien or *War and Peace*, particularly with a skillful choice of tunes. I do not have any scientific study results to cite, but I would have to think that it can lower blood pressure and reduce stress. It surely pumped me up before playing in a big game.

All that, and they do not even require a childproof cap.

Give me some headphones and a little bit of solitude—it's like joy in stereo.

Rebounding, by Beth

As a previous essay detailed, I am a big fan of lifting weights—it is something I enjoy doing. My workout routines change somewhat frequently, but lately I have noticed a trend. My days allotted to lifting weights remain constant each week, but the number of days I spend doing cardio conditioning continues to decrease. Most weeks, as I am writing this, it is only once or twice a week that I take the time to get my heart pumping. Seeing that fact on the screen in front of me is causing me to come under conviction; I need to step it up in this area.

I used to be much more diligent with cardio conditioning. I would get in the prescribed thirty to forty-five minutes five days a week, as well as play tennis multiple days each week. Although I know aerobic conditioning is good for my physical health as well as my mental health, I have never enjoyed the process very much.

We currently have a stair climber, rower, and recumbent bike. In the past we had a treadmill that I logged many miles on as well. I am also open to taking walks outside when the weather is conducive—not too hot and not too cold. As my husband would explain it, I have a small window of comfort. My at-home options together with our gym membership provide me with enough alternatives to keep me interested. In theory this may be true, but in my reality, it does not feel that way.

Temperature issues aside, walking outside is the most enjoyable thing for me of these choices. Sometimes I walk with Gary, sometimes with a friend or friends, and often alone. Where we currently live, my walks take place in the neighborhood next to ours. It is a large neighborhood with hills and sidewalks. The streets are tree lined, and the homes are welcoming, at least in my imagination. I like to listen to music or podcasts as I watch the scenery change before my eyes, sometimes pausing to take in a particularly beautiful flower, tree, or view of the sky.

About a year ago, I rediscovered another form of cardio that I hadn't done in years: rebounding. In case you don't know, rebounding is using a personal-sized version of a trampoline to jump up and down like a child. Perhaps that is why I find this type of cardio so much fun. Although there are videos and teaching on the best way to get a good workout on this equipment, I do my own thing and just have fun.

With the music playing loudly, I spin, jump, kick, and twist until any tangled-up thoughts or troubles of the day are shaken from my head. If I feel the need to vent some frustrations, I set the rebounder up next to our punching bag, and suddenly I am a fighter in the ring. Although I'm sure I look like nothing close to what I envision, in my mind I am dancing like a prize fighter as I practice uppercuts, hooks, and jabs. Thankfully we have blinds on our windows, so I can check my inhibitions at the door: what happens in our workout room stays in our workout room.

If the goal of my cardio workout is to get my heart rate up and sweat some toxins out of my system, then my rebounder workout might deserve a B. If the goal is to have fun, allow myself to act like a kid, and let the cares of the day fall by the wayside, then my rebounder workout deserves an A-plus.

Going to the Farmers Market, by Tara

A friend of mine once told me about a game she played with her mother as a child. It was a simple game, but really quite brilliant. During the weekly visit to the grocery store, my friend was permitted to pick out one item to purchase and take home. Of course, most children would opt for a sugary cereal, something from the candy aisle, or an otherwise unhealthy product purposefully adorned in bright, attention-grabbing colors and placed at a child's eye level, so there were stipulations. First, the selected item could only reside in the vegetable or fruit categories of the food pyramid. Second, each item had to be something new, something my friend had never seen or tasted before. Upon bringing the groceries home, my friend and her mother would then work together to learn how to wash, cut, and prepare the produce as either an ingredient in or the basis of a meal. Sometimes their creations worked, and other times they were downright disgusting, but my friend recalls that it was *always* fun.

What probably began as a way to appease a bored child and alleviate the endless stream of "Can we get this?" and "Can we get that?" became an integral part of my friend's upbringing. This simple tradition she shared with her mother instilled in her a culinary curiosity and openness, as well as offered a special way for a mother and daughter to bond.

Aside from planning to steal this clever and adorable tradition one day and use as my own with my offspring (I totally will), I oftentimes am reminded of my friend's story. It happens mostly when I visit the market.

The Dekalb Farmers Market, an expansive world market in Atlanta, is comparative to Disney World for the culinarily inclined. You could get lost for hours behind those doors, simply perusing every specialized section. There is a section for oils and seasonings, fine wines, every variety of fruit and vegetable you could possibly imagine, cheeses imported from all over the world, and live crab, catfish, and lobsters that you can hand select and take home. There are beautiful flowers and plants, fresh breads ranging from sourdough to croissants, and even a pocket dedicated to housing various types of coffee beans that you can have ground in-house. It's truly a foodie's playground.

I'm no foodie—I'm really not all that adventurous with my meals—but I find it easy to get caught up in the excitement of exploration at the Dekalb Market. A thirty-minute drive from my apartment, going to the market is less of a quick trip and more of a planned excursion. It is more downtime than an errand, a leisurely stroll rather than a hurried tromp up and down grocery store aisles to scoop up products and cross off items on a sloppily penned list.

When I visit the market, I think about my friend, and I encourage myself to be open minded. I pick up interesting-looking produce, read about cheeses from Denmark and Germany, and investigate the various oils and grains. I try to take home something new, but even if I don't, I think it's simply about being able to take my time, be mindful about the things I put in my body, and enjoy the trip. Really, what makes those trips so enjoyable isn't what's purchased at the market, but what the market represents. Just like my friend and her mother's game, it's the experience that matters the most.

> **Blessed is everyone who fears the Lord, who walks in his ways! You shall eat the fruit of the labor of your hands; you shall be blessed, and it shall be well with you.**
> **—Psalm 128:1–2 (ESV)**

Walk-Off Hits, by Gary

Anyone who has ever played or watched baseball or softball knows the spontaneous explosion of joy that occurs when your team pushes across the winning run on a walk-off hit.

The term *walk-off* derives from the effect on the players as the game is suddenly over—there is not much sense in hanging around on the field. Unfortunately, like a well-known law of physics, one team's joy has the equal and opposite reaction on the losing team.

Considering that those who compete understand it is in the nature of sports for there to be winners and losers, as well as the well-worn consolation "we'll get 'em next time," our focus here is on the feeling of elation.

It is important to point out, though, that not every walk-off is created equal. Although scoring the winning run in the bottom of the eleventh inning is great, it does not compare to turning a deficit into a victory with a three-run homer with two outs in the bottom of the ninth. The latter borders on ecstasy.

The magnitude of the excitement might also relate to the circumstances. For instance, the level of endorphins released from winning the fifth game of the season is likely quite a bit less than the mad rush felt in the fifth game of the play-offs.

In 2009, I was extremely fortunate to be at Philadelphia's Citizens Bank Park for game four of the National League championship series, pitting the Los Angeles Dodgers against my beloved Phillies. I saw both scenarios play out when Jimmy Rollins smashed a two-out, ninth-inning double against one of the top relief pitchers in baseball to turn a defeat into victory.

The entire stadium erupted. Players ran around the field celebrating, and forty-seven thousand fans danced and screamed as if they had won the lottery. When the winning run slid across the plate, an unknown woman next to me and I looked at each other—and spontaneously embraced!

It was a sports memory to last a lifetime. Perhaps the only way it could have been more joyful is if the walk-off hit came off my own bat.

CHAPTER 9
Sensing Joy

Faith, by Gary

Two job candidates competing for the same position speak to a cab driver on the way to an interview. Brad tells the driver, "I doubt if I will get the job." When Mike climbs into the same cab an hour later, he tells the driver, "My background and experience make me a good fit for the job."

Which candidate do you think has the greatest chance to land the job? It is unclear whether Mike is actually better suited for the position, but outlook matters.

One of the most-read books of all time is Norman Vincent Peale's classic *The Power of Positive Thinking*. This book has motivated and transformed lives for generations by helping readers understand that expectations and approach impact results.

Clearly, there are many benefits to operating with a glass-half-full mentality. Mike's mind-set likely projected confidence in the interview, a valued quality. Conversely, Brad's half-empty outlook could be overheard from two conference rooms over and ensured that he did not have them at hello. No matter how brilliant his points or comments during the interview, Brad arrived casting a "no" vote for himself.

Simply focusing on the positives rather than the negatives changes your own perception of any experience. Friends immediately come to mind who fall on either end of the spectrum. Whether going to an event or restaurant together, some friends gleefully await an enjoyable time to enfold. On the other hand, we have friends who show up with figurative forensic tools to seek out grievances, flaws, and problems.

I know this for certain—hanging out with the former is much more relaxing and enjoyable. And is there any doubt which end of the spectrum is routinely experiencing happiness and joy?

Faith is a step—or giant leap—past simple positive thinking. It is the power of positive thinking with a reason.

Positive thinking is a bit of a one-way street. It is somewhat unilateral in nature. A push, if you will. By expecting good things, the odds increase that the actual outcomes will fall that way. Anticipating less favorable results often becomes a self-fulfilling prophecy.

Faith, on the other hand, is bilateral, running both directions. It is a push and a pull. You can expect good things because you have God on the other side, who tells us, "Trust in the Lord with all your heart, and lean not on your own understanding. Submit to Him in all your ways, and He will make your paths straight."

In general, the bridge from a positive demeanor to joy is much shorter than the arduous journey from negativity. One is a short jaunt, while the other is a cross-state trek uphill.

Tackling daily life with a positive disposition, especially considering an upshot of more favorable outcomes, allows you to live on the edge of joy.

It doesn't stop there, though. It gets even better. Faith by grace fills you with an undeniable feeling of peace and joy regardless of the circumstances around you. Now that is living!

> **Jesus replied, "What is impossible with man is possible with God."**
> **—Luke 18:27 (NIV)**

Escaping Monotony with a Bouquet of Flowers, by Tara

It is far too easy for life to become monotonous and muted. It is far too easy to fall into a routine, to chase comfort, to find stability in familiarity. When our lives are defined by routines, that's when we see the pages of the stories of our lives fly by like a paperback book flapping in the wind. What was at one time exciting and sizzling and new becomes a series of mundane routines necessary to the upkeep of a normal, day-to-day life.

When I graduated college, I immediately was whisked away into the workforce. It was a whirlwind of walking across the stage to receive my diploma, stuffing my belongings in garbage bags, and cruising along the interstate to a brand-new city and home. It was new beginnings, new environments, new friends, and new routines. It was adapting to adulthood, teaching myself how to cook, and finding genuine excitement in budget sheets and client meetings. New is exciting. It is easy to find joy in what's new.

I think it's when we fall into a routine that life can become dull. We find ourselves doing the same things every day, every week, every month, because our lives are defined by those routines. We set our alarms for 7:15 a.m., brew medium-roast coffee to sip in traffic, and settle in at our desks with our spreadsheets and 153 unread e-mails. We eat brown-bagged sandwiches when our stomachs begin to growl, and we watch time slow down as we eagerly await the hour hand passing the five. When the sun has dipped below the horizon, we pick up our children from daycare, or pay a visit to the gym, or hurry home to cook a meal for our families. We do laundry on Sundays, buy groceries on Mondays, wash the dishes on Tuesdays, take the garbage out on Wednesdays, and vacuum the floors on Thursdays. We live for the weekends, when we have a glimmer of hope that we will live out the exciting plans we have drawn up in our heads all week long. When Friday rolls around, we are exhausted. Over time, the skip in our step slows, the sparkle in our eye fades, and the melodic hum of life becomes an overplayed tune.

There have been periods of time when I have succumbed to the mundane repetitions of life. I have allowed myself to become bored, allowed the weeks to fly by, and then wondered what happened to the last two months of my life. This is not how God wants us to live our lives.

God desires joy and exuberance for his children. He does not want the sparkle in our eyes to ever fade. He wants us to have an unquenchable thirst for life and love. I believe God wants us to sing in the shower, skip along the sidewalks, find satisfaction in our work, notice the birds and the flowers and the breeze, and find joy in everything, even in something as trivial as the sweet, juicy tanginess of the first bite of a tangerine.

When I feel that the pages of my life's story are flying by, when I feel like I'm in a gray, muted rut, when life loses its luster, I buy a bouquet of flowers at the grocery store. Nothing fancy—just an inexpensive bouquet of grapefruit-colored spray roses or perky, amethyst-purple tulips. I bring home the flowers with my usual order of eggs, bread, and milk and arrange them on my windowsill in a transparent, cylindrical vase that I purchased at Goodwill. Over the next week, I wake up to the sight of beautiful flowers and inhale the fresh fragrance they exude. With that, with one small addition to my routine, my life suddenly feels exciting, radiant, and new again. I'm reminded of the little things, the little joys that are so easily overlooked, and I recover the skip in my step again.

JOY ALL AROUND US

Nativities, by Beth

My mother-in-law has always loved Christmas and all the traditions that surround it. From what I have been told by my husband, she came by this naturally, as her mother was the same way. I believe in a lot of ways this has also been passed down to Gary. You might be thinking, don't most people enjoy the traditions of Christmas, including gift giving, decorating, making cookies, and time with family? To a certain degree, this may be true, but I believe some people have a supercharged love for the season, and therefore the traditions in their homes are celebrated to a greater extent.

This truth is evident at my mother-in-law's house on Christmas morning as a multitude of gifts overflows the living room. It is even more evident by the quantity of holiday decorations that begin to fill her home starting in early December. The decorations include collections of Santas, angels, and Byers' Choice dolls representing Dickens's *A Christmas Carol*. A tree sits in the corner of their living room decorated with more angels and white lights. Additional trees are set up in her family room and kitchen. Christmas artwork is placed on the walls. Pillows and throws in seasonal colors are arranged on couches and chairs. Holiday-themed plates and glasses are retrieved from the recesses of the dining hutch to await special meals. Decorations continue into the upstairs area, including the hall bathroom and guest room where we stay. At my in-laws' home, we brush our teeth next to a small Christmas tree and fall asleep under a Christmas-themed bedspread. My mother-in-law also has a collection of holiday attire and jewelry to enjoy as she counts down the days until December 25. I could go on for a few more paragraphs, but by now you have an appreciation for her commitment to the season.

I grew up in a home where we loved celebrating and getting together with family, but the decorations at our house were simple and far from numerous. We had a tree and a small collection of various Christmas-themed tabletop decorations. We cuddled up with the same knitted afghan throughout the entire year, and our special meals were served on plain white china. One of my favorite decorations was our nativity scene. It was beautiful and old, having originally been used at our church. It was acquired by our family at a church fundraiser when the church no longer had use for it. My father made a wooden stable to hold the figurines, and we added straw to it each year before setting up the scene. My mother had no problem with me playing with these breakable pieces, and I remember well my fascination with the baby Jesus.

My husband and I have settled into a holiday rhythm that lies somewhere between our childhood family homes. We admittedly have many more decorations than my parents' home but far fewer than Gary's. Like both sides, however, we emphasize family get-togethers and spending time with people we love. The decorations in our home have helped us create memories and traditions as we celebrate this very special time of the year.

I purchased the first nativity for our family soon after we were married. It has beautiful muted colors and a wooden stable. As a child, Tara was given the responsibility to set up this display each year. I enjoyed watching her carefully unwrap each piece from its protective layer of tissue paper and place it in the perfect location in the stable. She took her time, until the scene in front of her matched the one she was seeing with her mind's eye. Admittedly I was thankful when each precious piece was unpacked and set in place with no casualties. Unlike my childhood home, in our house, playing with the nativity was not allowed.

When my parents were starting to downsize, they offered up their nativity to whoever in the family might want it. I could only dare to hope I would be able to receive this family heirloom. Yet thankfully, none of my siblings were interested. I excitedly headed home one day with an old shoe box of my father's that contained these treasures. Now that both of my parents are gone, it is even more precious to me. And although my normal organizing tendencies would encourage me to store these nativity pieces in one of my many clear plastic boxes, my heart does not allow me to transfer them out of their home in my father's shoe box except for their annual unveiling and display.

About three years ago, I saw a nativity scene created by an artist that was truly unique. The holy family was designed in a reverent way, but the other pieces were colorful and a bit whimsical. I immediately fell in love with it. With gift catalog in hand, I showed Gary and gave him a not-so-subtle hint that I might like to start collecting this new nativity. With Christmas fast approaching, I was hoping he could use some gift ideas. Since that time, we have collected most of the pieces, and this display has become the featured nativity in our home.

Although I am grateful for our newest nativity, my reasons for wanting it are not about acquiring another collection of holiday decorations. For our family, the most important thing about Christmas is reflecting on God's love and His goodness toward us as we spend time with family and friends. Nativity scenes are such a tangible and beautiful picture of God's love and His plan to create a family, His family, through the birth of His son. It gives me so much joy to unpack these beautiful treasures each year and remember how blessed I am for what He did for me so that I can be a part of His family.

> **For to us a child is born, to us a son is given, and the government will be on his shoulders. And he will be called Wonderful Counselor, Mighty God, Everlasting Father, Prince of Peace.**
> **—Isaiah 9:6 (NIV)**

Food, by Gary

At its most basic level, food provides sustenance in our lives. It is the fuel that powers our bodily engines. Like the air around us, without it, we can neither function nor live.

While our bodies unconsciously breathe by reflexively drawing oxygen into our lungs, we must choose and act to consume food. As additional testimony to our perfect design, we are naturally compelled to eat, as food is one of the most fundamental pleasures in life.

Actually, for many, food is one of the *greatest* pleasures in life. There is a reason that it is central to most family and social events, celebrations, holiday gatherings, and parties. Breaking bread together has long been the preferred accompanying activity to get to know others, whether it's a first date, a business meeting, or simple fellowship.

Food is also often the way we show love to others. My mother has demonstrated this practice through lovingly preparing gastro delights for friends and family since my earliest memories. From impromptu gatherings to well-planned meals, Mimi has taken considerable joy in serving up culinary joy to others. Others might similarly exhibit love through a particular specialty niche, such as the art of grilling, baking pastries, or whipping up an edible welcome mat in the form of a key lime pie for the new neighbors. (For northerners, please substitute apple streusel cake or cherry pie at your discretion.)

While speaking of my mother, it is worth noting that she has rarely allowed a family gathering to slip by without having a simple meal turn into a feast. We have keenly observed that she has a few enabling tricks up her sleeve, such as the notion that abundant quantities maximize satisfaction and multiply the days of enjoyment. Also, it would seem that a couple particular ingredients may perhaps add the secret to the sauce—namely, butter and sugar.

From our earliest days of dating, Beth was often amused at my family's love affair with food. She would find the detailed accounts we might provide of recent dining experiences or reminiscing about our favorite foods a bit humorous. This was largely foreign to her, but for me, enjoying food was a way of life.

In fact, it was a huge part of life that took center stage on holidays, vacations, and pretty much anytime we got together with friends and family.

JOY ALL AROUND US

Although her strong-gust-of-wind-could-blow-her-away appearance still belies it, the joy of food has long made its way into Beth's heart. The snickers have been supplanted by similar appreciation and joy.

When people ask me about my food tastes, I often feel compelled to trot out the stale line about being on a "see food" diet—for the unfamiliar few, my tendency is to eat pretty much whatever I see. Although it may usually coax a grudging laugh, my motivation for describing it that way is that it might be the best description of my relationship with food.

For as far back as my cognitive memory will take me, I have had a deep romance with food. Although my tastes may have evolved through the years, it's funny how this is a mostly additive phenomenon. By that I mean, newly acquired tastes and discovered foods are simply added to the "yes" side of the culinary ledger. Other than my own choices not to consume something for health or some other personal reason (think fried butter, fettuccini Alfredo, or rabbit) I am hard-pressed to identify foods stricken from the list.

Once (with particular emphasis on the singularity), I unknowingly enjoyed a buffet item with a place card labeled in French, only to learn later that the dish in question happened to be frogs' legs. As you might imagine, my subsequently adopted food-consumption protocol now calls for English interpretation and key-ingredient disclosure. This particular food now resides on my brief but etched-in-stone "thanks, but no thanks" list.

The less pleasurable experiences aside, there is little doubt that one of the greatest pleasures throughout my life continues to be food. At times, consuming my favorite foods evokes even loftier emotions. For me, and surely many others, biting into a hot slice of one of my favorite brands of pizza brings joy.

Upon reflection, the list of foods that bring joy is almost endless—perhaps infinite when you consider the boundless combinations of ingredients and preparation methods. Classic dishes to nouveau cuisine, old favorites to new recipes, hot to cold, appetizers to desserts—the list of foods that thrill the taste buds is extensive and wide ranging.

I'm both a traditionalist and an explorer in search of the next great culinary delight. It's difficult to improve on Italian mainstays such as spaghetti and meatballs with red sauce or gravy, lasagna, chicken Parmesan, or eggplant Parmesan. In fact, as accentuated with the repetition, the "Parmesan" part makes almost anything delightful.

Although I enjoy roast beef, meat loaf, and turkey, the real truth is that these carnivorous mainstays provide a conduit to an even greater joy—mashed potatoes. My family will surely attest to the obscene portions of mashed potatoes that have routinely graced my plate over the years. And speaking of turkey, did I mention stuffing?

Classic recipes and foods aside, I am always happy to try new twists, combining foods and tastes in creative ways. For this reason, I particularly enjoy dining at restaurants offering unique dishes invented and whipped up by right-brain-powered chefs. Entrees prepared with imaginative combinations of ingredients and flavors read like poetry on the menu and turn into song with every bite.

A traditional club sandwich well satisfies, but a creative blend of foods artfully layered onto a flavorful roll quenches the appetite of adventure and enjoyment. Sometimes sheer simplicity, such as a tomato sandwich, argues that less is more. Savoring the perfection of tasty, thick slices of tomatoes in peak season with nothing but salt, pepper, and mayo on toast offers simple joy. Alternatively, you really can't go wrong by adding a couple ingredient letters to make it a BLT.

For many, dessert offers the greatest culinary enjoyment. It is usually eaten last to send everyone off on a high note or even reserved to enjoy on its own a little later. Whatever your treat of choice, joy is savored with each mouthful until the very last bite. Thinking of my personal favorite, joy is striking the perfect balance in taking enough time to savor an ice cream cone without the heartache of seeing it literally slip through your fingers.

First published in 1931, the classic book *Joy of Cooking* is now approaching thirty million units sold and was named one of the most influential books of the twentieth century. Although cooking itself offers enjoyment, it would seem that the activity would be a bit empty without the actual joy of eating.

> **So go ahead. Eat your food with joy, and drink your wine with a happy heart, for God approves of this!**
> **—Ecclesiastes 9:7 (NLT)**

Persevering through Adversity, by Gary

Yesterday was "one of those days." We have all had them. They are few and far between in some periods—but all too frequent other times.

Most of yesterday involved a lot of wasted motion with little to show for it. In the morning, I spent a couple hours working on a very detailed online application submission. Unfortunately, that time was rendered meaningless when I received an error message and all my data input was wiped out.

Rather than repeat the whole process again, I placed a call to see if my data could be recovered. After leaving a voice mail, I decided to shift my attention to another item on my to-do list.

A previous employer was discontinuing management of retirement plans, so I needed to open a new IRA elsewhere to roll over the funds. In the interest of simplicity, I decided to open the account with a well-known online bank/broker where we had an existing relationship.

The process was quick and easy. I recall thinking how happy I was with my decision to go it alone online as I breezed to the final step—reviewing the data for final submission. Everything looked good, so I clicked on the "submit" button.

Much to my dismay, rather than receiving a "Congratulations, your account is now open!" message, I received one of those broad error messages that cites a potential problem covering everything from a format issue with any of the data fields to your operating system to solar flares. About an hour later, after checking and rechecking everything, resubmitting approximately seventy times, and engaging customer service via chat, the agent concluded that I needed to use another browser and start over again.

This presented a perfect time to step away and run an errand to pick up an item at the store. The thirty-minute drive would allow me to defuse pent-up frustrations. Unfortunately, after I had arrived at the store and waited awhile, it was determined that I could not pick up the item until the next day.

At that point, my only reaction was a brief chuckle and the decision to try again tomorrow. When I returned to my office, I decided to restart my quest for the new IRA. After more error messages and another lengthy chat session, I rejected a suggestion to try a convoluted approach to create a new customer ID, but I asked the agent to wipe out all my application data so I could start over from the beginning.

Lo and behold, this worked, and I received the coveted congratulatory message. Feeling a hot streak, I turned my attention back to the original failed application submission. Two for two! I even figured out a little shortcut.

You are probably searching hard to understand what joy might be found in this series of events. The answer is that the joy came at the end when I finally did have success!

Persevering through life's challenges (and in this case, life's little challenges) with an unrelenting tenacity makes success that much more enjoyable. This is especially true when you do it with the right spirit and maintain good cheer.

No matter what you call them—challenges, difficulties, trials, or tribulations—these adversities provide a sharp backdrop to feel the joy in succeeding. Without adversity, would we even recognize the emotion?

> **Consider it pure joy, my brothers and sisters, whenever you face trials of many kinds, because you know that the testing of your faith produces perseverance. Let perseverance finish its work so that you may be mature and complete, not lacking anything.**
> **—James 1:2–4 (NIV)**

Handmade Gifts, by Beth

Our daughter, Tara, is both creative and gifted artistically. When she was a little girl, she started the tradition of making Christmas presents for our extended family. To make it simple, she gave the same gift to each family. Each year she would start thinking about what gift she was going to make sometime in November. She would page through craft catalogs and visit our local craft stores to get gift ideas. As she was an independent child, she didn't require much of my input to guide her as she decided what to give each year. Some years, I do remember thinking, *I hope this isn't too much for her to take on.* Thankfully she always managed to get her gifts completed and wrapped in time to pack for our annual trip to the frozen tundra. This locale, although normally referred to as Philadelphia, garnered its nickname soon after we relocated to the warm Carolinas.

When Tara started this tradition as a young grade-schooler, she would select a craft kit that could be assembled from the provided materials. One year it was an assortment of Christmas ornaments featuring marshmallow snowmen doing various holiday-themed activities. As she got older, she made and designed the gifts on her own, no kits required. As a teen, she started to develop a love for photography, and photo books or calendars replaced the homemade craft gifts.

My father also gave family members handmade gifts. As one of his hobbies was woodworking, his gifts were formed on a lathe, then carefully sanded and stained by hand. These gifts were sometimes as intricate as grandfather clocks (usually reserved for weddings) and sometimes as simple as wooden bowls. Jewelry boxes were made for all the females in our family. Child-size chairs, toy cars, and marble mazes were given to his grandchildren. My parents' home was filled with many of my father's creations. Clocks showcasing his talent adorned the walls. Bowls he crafted were displayed on tables also constructed by him. In the kitchen you would find a banana tree, numerous trays, and a random toy car or two, all lovingly made by his hands.

My father passed away two months prior to his ninetieth birthday. We were planning to celebrate with a big party for our extended family. He was planning to celebrate by giving each of his guests a handmade gift, a small bowl.

As I have watched the exchanging of gifts in our family through the years, it seems evident, especially with homemade gifts, that the giver's joy is equal to and often greater than that of the receiver. Lest anyone think this is because these handmade gifts are somehow inferior and not appreciated, let me set the record straight—these gifts were always greatly treasured by their recipients. The truth resides in something Jesus said: "It is more blessed and brings greater joy to give than to receive." I believe both my father and my daughter know this truth very well.

JOY ALL AROUND US

Blissful Refuge, by Gary

For most of my life, I had never experienced having a screened-in porch. That changed eighteen months ago when we moved into a new home.

At various times, my wife and I have debated whether we would want a screened-in porch. We considered this feature when moving or as a renovation to our then-existing home. Our conversation unfortunately always landed on foregoing it, mostly because it blocked the natural light that we loved streaming into our home.

All I can say is that I never knew what I was missing.

Our current home already incorporated a screened-in porch into the design. We loved everything about the house, so my wife and I decided it was time to find out the right answer to our debate.

This has undoubtedly become my favorite place to hang out.

After many years of heading to the office every day, I now work from home. This is a luxury worth its own essay, but one of the great benefits is that it affords me much more time on the porch. Although I have a highly functional and comfortable office in our home, I have set up shop on the porch.

Living in the Southeast, we enjoy warmth for an extended portion of the year, so you can pretty much find me on the porch most days from breakfast to dinnertime, spring through fall. A laptop, power strip, and basket of desk essentials have become my "portable office," which is complete when merged with our high-top table on the porch.

Adding to my joyful bliss is that some of my very best friends accompany me most of the time. More specifically, the porch has also become our cats' favorite hangout spot as well. It is the perfect locale to soak in the sun, watch the birds and squirrels, and enjoy a cool breeze in the shade on a hot day. (I also like to believe that hanging with me is an added attraction.)

Besides my own ability to take in nature's splendor as I gaze into our backyard from my high-top perch, the atmosphere is further enhanced by my favorite music quietly playing in the background. (The quiet part admittedly changes from time to time as my top tunes collide with an opportune moment.)

A controlled environment, protected from the elements, with sun, shade, breeze, nature, music, and companionship (as well as a direct shot to the kitchen), offers a little glimpse of paradise. I am not sure who loves the screened-in porch more—the cats or me—but I do know that it brings us all many hours of joy!

Pizza, by Gary

Our family's favorite pizza on the planet is found on the boardwalk in Ocean City, New Jersey. Signage spelling out "Manco and Manco Pizza" in old-time movie theater lights fronts the otherwise nondescript pizza shops.

Don't be fooled by the little wooden booths, round vinyl stools at the counter, or the limited menu on the wall—this place richly deserves having its name written in lights like a 1950s movie star!

When I say that it is our family's favorite pizza, I mean every single person in our extended family. Like any family, it is hard to get everyone to totally agree on anything, but when it comes to Manco and Manco, the passion is shared by all.

After perhaps waiting in a lengthy line for a seat at one of these three popular pizza shops, you watch workers toss and spin dough, spill a special blend of cheeses on each pie, and finish them off with a quick squirt of the secret sauce. Your anticipation rises as the workers remove thin, perfectly cooked, bubbly disks from the rotating ovens and slice them with the precision of a plastic surgeon.

You watch intently to see if the latest pie is coming your way, only to see it delivered somewhat cruelly to another table. When the moment arrives that the waiter heads your way, only some quick self-talk prevents you from losing all manners and decorum by diving in before everyone is served.

The first bite confirms that it was worth every second of anticipation—as well as several months of cravings and a two-and-a-half-hour drive. This is the best pizza on the planet!

Whether it's Manco and Manco or some other place, most everyone has their favorite brand of pizza. It does not take much thought to understand why someone coined the phrase "a little slice of heaven."

JOY ALL AROUND US

CHAPTER 10
Joy Shining Down

Joy under Our Nose, by Beth

Memories are often triggered by our senses, as we find ourselves briefly in another place or time while our bodies are experiencing the here and now. We pass a mother with a newborn swaddled against her chest, and we are taken back in time to when our own children were new to this world. We hear an old song on the radio, and we find ourselves at a middle school dance, waiting for an invitation from our then-current crush. We smell a pie baking in the oven, and we are transported to our parents' dining room table surrounded by friends and family. Of course not all memories take us to a good place, but when they do, it is fun to linger a bit and recapture some of the joy these places hold in our lives.

For me, my sense of smell seems to be most directly connected to my memories. I don't even need to smell something naturally to help me make the trip down memory lane. In my mind I am able to vividly recall and experience certain odors from my younger years. Freshly mimeographed paper and the distinctive plastic smell of Barbies are two that come to mind. Neither of these smells is inherently pleasant, but bound together with the memory each evokes, they translate into a sweet source of joy.

Another smell that resonates strongly with me, both now and from my past, is the smell of lilacs. The love of this sweet spring flower was planted in me as a young girl as I visited my grandmother's home. My grandmother lived in an old farmhouse where a beautiful and massive lilac tree stood next to the garage. I can remember as a child standing under the blossoms and inhaling deeply this heavenly smell. I can picture the soft pale color of the lilacs mingled among the green leaves with the backdrop of a cloud-filled sky of blue above. Even now as I drive down country roads in the springtime, I am tempted to trespass as I see lilacs waiting to be picked, so wanting to take them home to enjoy their fragrance.

Joy produced from our senses is not of course only for looking back. Our senses allow us to more vividly experience our world and all it has to offer today. What a blessing that our Creator designed our bodies to experience and interact with our environment in multiple ways. Often our experiences are shared and enjoyed with others around us, as we walk past the open door of a bakery or hand in hand watch the sun set from our front porch.

For some the joy produced by our sense of smell is as simple as the aroma of coffee steaming from our cup in the morning, a special meal waiting in the oven upon our arrival home, or the scent of our youngest child freshly bathed and awaiting story time.

The sound of a loved one on the other end of our cell phone after a long, hard day and the melody of our new favorite song emanating from the car stereo as we face a long commute both do much to usher in joy and send away negative emotions.

The comfort of a warm embrace when the world seems overwhelming and the feel of a little child's arms around our leg both remind us that we are not alone. We are strengthened and comforted by these sweet blessings of touch as we realize our gratitude and love for our friends and family.

Seeing our child's face entering the kitchen after school or our pet's lively or sometimes indifferent greeting when we arrive home allows us to step outside of ourselves and share life with those around us. Our sense of sight allows us to communicate with one another through the written word as well as enjoy the beauty all around us created by both God and man.

All our senses are a blessing and a source of joy in our lives. They add a depth to our experiences in this world that takes us from black and white to Technicolor. Oftentimes they are taken for granted, but when circumstance limit them, they are sorely missed. They allow us to enjoy and savor the world around us in a way that is limited only by our own neglect and indifference. Perhaps one of the secrets to finding more joy in our lives is truly found by stopping to smell the roses, as well as really looking at the roses, then grabbing a large pizza and sitting down close to a loved one and enjoying our roses and pizza together!

Putting a Smile on Someone's Face, by Gary

Have you ever encountered someone whose face, body language, and even actions seemed to scream that they were having a bad day? This, of course, is a bit of a rhetorical question, as we all experience this pretty regularly, whether it is the receptionist at the doctor's office, an overly aggressive driver, a neighbor taking out the trash, or a loved one.

The other day our garage door seemed to have a mind of its own as the cable somehow became entangled and pulled the door off the tracks. Although the ability to fix things is not high on my list of blessings, my ego led me to grab a ladder to diagnose the necessary repair. As I searched for the correct lug wrench, my wife had a better idea and called a repairman.

She greeted him when he arrived about an hour later and let me know that he warned the door might fall onto our car if I did not move it immediately. When I walked out to talk to him, he was clearly having one of those days. Adding insult to the pounding sun in what seemed like 110-degree heat, he blurted out, "I don't know why these emergencies always happen late on a Friday afternoon!" As tersely as the words landed, his scowl and fatigued body told even more of the story.

I replied, "Yes, sorry about the timing…it's Murphy's Law. We really appreciate you coming out late on a Friday afternoon." After he grumbled a little more and questioned what we might have done, I assured him that my wife caught it right away and we immediately stopped trying to operate the door.

I proceeded to engage him in a conversation about the time our garage door coil snapped on a Friday night as we went to head out on vacation, delaying us a day with our car trapped in the garage. As we talked more about his day, his mood started to lift. By the time the door was fixed, he was smiling, telling us stories, and showing us pictures on his cell phone.

There is no doubt that the garage door repairman had a much more difficult day than I did, but it made me feel a real sense of happiness that he was going to start his weekend with a smile on his face.

By the way, he advised me that my approach to fixing the door would have resulted in a trip to the hospital. Perhaps the Holy Spirit whispered in my wife's ear to make the call, and a guardian angel pushed the repairman to make one more stop after a long, hard day.

> **Gratitude can transform common days into thanksgivings, turn routine jobs into joy, and change ordinary opportunities into blessings.**
> **—William Arthur Ward**

Rainbows, by Gary

A recent event pulled this phenomenon of nature to the forefront of my mind, but rainbows have long had a special place in our family. Our daughter, Tara, showed a keen fascination and appreciation for them from a very early age.

By nature, rainbows are elusive and largely unpredictable. Surely, we know the probability of spotting one increases when weather conditions are right, but just as surely, it is hit or miss.

Tara's delight with rainbows caused our family to instinctively search the sky whenever there was a confluence of sun and rain in hopeful anticipation of spotting a glorious arc across the sky.

There was always an extra measure of excitement to be the first to point it out for others to see. My wife became particularly adept at spotting a budding rainbow and took joy in guiding Tara's eyes to the glorious fruit of nature—which in turn imparted excitement and joy to her.

Although Tara now lives in another city, muscle memory and thought conditioning still trigger my wife and me to lift our eyes skyward when the elements are right. My guess is that Tara's reactions remain very similar.

Rainbows themselves are truly glorious and joyful in nature. Besides traversing magnificently across the sky in a perfectly formed arc, they display the color spectrum in brilliant, gradient bands.

When rainbows form, they are absolute in design. Although the size and brilliance may vary, they do not form randomly in assorted shapes and colors.

Besides the obvious visceral appeal, rainbows offer an even better reason for joy. The scriptures tell us that God created them as a demonstration of His commitment and faithfulness to us.

Every occurrence is a glorious handwritten message from our Heavenly Father Himself. Is it any wonder that spotting one evokes feelings of wonder and joy?

A few days ago, while driving to another city, I prayed out loud for about fifteen minutes. In closing, I asked God to continue to reveal His wonderful presence around us. Moments later, a budding rainbow caught my eye in the sky to my left and continued to build in intensity over the next few minutes as I drove. Just as the rainbow reached a brilliance and saturation that I have never witnessed before, I noticed that the arc seemed to end on top of a billboard to my right.

This was not just any billboard, either—it featured a twenty-foot-high painting of Jesus!

As I passed the billboard, the rainbow began to fade, disappearing altogether after a few miles. Still somewhat in awe, when I anxiously phoned my wife to tell her, it was not on my mind what I had prayed immediately prior to the sighting. On my drive home later that evening as I reflected on the spectacular aerial display earlier, I finally realized that the rainbow was exactly what I had requested in the closing of my prayer.

Two days later, several photographers snapped shots of a glorious rainbow in New York City that made world news. Besides verbal accounts of its stunning magnificence, the date and placement added great significance. You see, this particular rainbow appeared on the eve of the fourteenth anniversary of the 9/11 attacks and seemed to originate from the Freedom Tower, which was erected on the site of the fallen World Trade Center towers!

Needless to say, as much as they already had significance in our family, I will never look at rainbows quite the same way again.

When I see the rainbow in the clouds, I will remember the eternal covenant between God and every living creature on earth.
—Genesis 9:16 (NLT)

GARY SUESS, ELIZABETH SUESS & TARA SUESS

Baseball, by Gary

Baseball was my first love in the athletic realm. Considering the baseball permanently residing on my desk and baseball art displayed in my office, it would be fair to say that the sport still maintains a special place in my heart. It is unclear when this passion first came upon me, but it predated my ability to grip a baseball.

Perhaps the infatuation began with the purchase of my first pack of baseball cards. In addition to the stale stick of bubble gum that required some dental tenacity to soften up, each pack contained ten cards with major-league players in various poses and each player's statistics on the flip side. Some were action shots, some were glamorized poses, and some occasionally looked like they were unknowingly captured by the paparazzi—but all were prized possessions. Seeing these athletic warriors in cool uniforms surely made a good impression, but the back side of those cards also appealed to my burgeoning mathematical brain, as baseball is a statistician's paradise.

Unlike today, when you can watch every game on TV, only select games were broadcast at that time. Considering the scarcity, our family typically tuned in to every broadcast. Watching these athletes execute their skills in elaborate stadiums with tens of thousands in the stands bolstered the romantic appeal.

Despite a deeply flawed existence, this exposure drew my loyalty to the hometown Philadelphia Phillies. That strong affinity still exists despite my having relocated three times and landed more than five hundred miles away in Braves territory. The Phillies have accumulated the most losses of any team in Major League Baseball history, yet my passion for them is unwavering.

The valleys have only served to make the peaks that much sweeter. The infrequent occasions of success have provided great joy for faithful fans of the team. It surely highlights an important lesson in life: keeping the faith and persevering gracefully through adversity brings even greater joy.

The ingenious invention of Wiffle ball spawned many playing careers, including mine. Shortly after my baseball entrée through plastics, I graduated to the real thing, now that I was large and strong enough to toss a leather-covered baseball and swing a diminutive wooden bat.

My love for the game continued to grow, marked by an insatiable appetite to practice and play. I spent countless hours taking imaginary swings, tossing up and whacking Wiffle balls, and firing a rubber ball at a taped strike zone on the side of our house. Oh, how my parents hated that repetitive thud, not to mention the wide assortment of windows that I shattered with wayward Wiffle ball blasts off various homes in the neighborhood. (In my defense, the objective is not to just poke the ball forward, but rather to crush it as hard as possible.)

Starting with Little League Baseball, my career advanced through various levels to college and a few years beyond. My backyard Wiffle ball developed my batting skills, and those repetitive wall thuds spawned a pitching career.

Some of my most joyous memories took place on a baseball diamond. Sunny days, the smell of fresh-cut grass, and the incessant baseball-speak chatter painted the backdrop, but the action between the white lines was what it was all about. Firing fastballs past hitters, throwing curveballs that froze batters and evaded bats, smacking baseballs into open areas, or even better, over the outfield fence, all contributed to the good feelings, but the overriding joy came from team victory.

Part of the beauty of baseball lies in the meld of individual competition within a team sport. You win and lose as a team. By and large, everyone needs to work together to achieve success, yet it requires individual execution. Perhaps it can best be described as a game within a game.

At the core of the sport is the ongoing pitcher-batter battle. When you are standing in the batter's box on the receiving end of a ninety-mile-per-hour fastball, you are on your own. On the flip side, when you are on the pitcher's mound staring down the batter, it is mano a mano. Conversely, you have a team behind you trying to catch the ball on defense, and each player has his turn to contribute on offense.

Considering how players rely on each other to perform, not to mention that teammates reconvene in the dugout every half inning, baseball develops camaraderie. Between sunflower-seed shells and a variety of liquid matter spewing to the ground, there is surely plenty of time to bond. In addition, few other sports feature all your teammates actively shouting encouragement when it's your turn in the limelight. Individual success is met with high fives and sometimes collective joy.

Although one popular movie reinforced that "there is no crying in baseball," another touched on the emotional appeal of the sport. The 1989 hit film *Field of Dreams* caused many male moviegoers to oddly linger to view the credits—or perhaps to allow their eyes to dry.

Baseball serves as a metaphor for youthful innocence and an apple pie slice of American culture. The original dreams of many boys involved success on the baseball diamond, and the ultimate aspiration was to one day play in front of large crowds in those iconic stadiums. The sport also offers a sense of timelessness unlike others with a clock—hope prevails until the last out is recorded. It provides a connection from generation to generation.

I have no doubt, the memories and friendships forged from playing and following this sport will last a lifetime. It is also clear that I am not alone in possessing a sentimental pocket in my heart for baseball.

Sunny Days, by Gary

It is not exactly a news flash that most everyone finds sunny days uplifting. Of course, our daughter is a bit of a contrarian and finds particular comfort in rainy days. It is not that she dislikes sunny days, but she would be best to explain her affinity to soggy weather.

Back to the overwhelming majority—there is an abundance of reasons to prefer bright, sunny days. Outdoor sports and activities become possible when it is dry. Work commutes are easier and safer. Your hair remains the way you intended when you combed it in the morning. Air travel typically stays on schedule. Picking up coffee or lunch at the drive-through is less adventurous. I'm just scratching the surface here.

Of course, the same things could be said about cloudy days without precipitation, but there is a tangible difference when bright sunshine is entered into the mix. It seems that we are hardwired to enjoy it. There is a palpable sense of happiness and joy in sunlight.

I believe that God intended it that way. The reason might be as simple as the fact that He *is* the light.

With few exceptions, most would agree that all the activities above are simply more enjoyable when the sun is shining. It permeates our psyches. It lifts our mood. It puts a little extra bounce in our step. The penetrating rays seem to warm us to our souls. Soothing blue and golden streams of light replace gray and awaken everything around us.

This quickly became apparent to me many years ago when we relocated from the Northeast to the Southeast. Over the first few months, while commuting back and forth in advance of our official move, friends and family would inquire about my perception of Charlotte. There is a lot to love about that city, but the one thing that struck me the most was the abundance of sunny days.

I am thinking that "Carolina blue" *did* come out of the blue. Literally.

As much as I sensed a sensitivity to not overplay the appeal of Charlotte, I couldn't help but to highlight the uplifting effect of the frequent beautiful blue skies. Moving away from family, friends, and my beloved sports teams was difficult, but there is little doubt that the change in climate provided the largest check mark on the other side of the ledger.

Today, even short visits to northern climates have me longing for more sun. This is not to suggest anyone should feel discontent or unhappiness above the Mason-Dixon Line, but my internal body settings have been recalibrated to the South. It's like jet lag rooted in light rather than time.

Although perception is often everything, there is some science behind the mood-light phenomenon. Sunlight causes the production of endorphins, serotonin, and vitamin D—all known to stir good feelings.

I have never spent more than a couple weeks in perpetually sunny environs like San Diego, but I sometimes wonder if sunshine ever gets boring to the residents. My guess is that boredom never sets in, but perhaps they begin to take the sunshine for granted. A sunny day after months of darkness at the poles must be particularly uplifting, whereas it is more of the same in Southern California.

Similarly, rainy days serve to make you appreciate and cherish sunny days that much more. I feel blessed to be in the Carolinas, where the less frequent gray days are overwhelmed by days lit and warmed by the radiant sun—but not so much that I lose the sense of joy from soaking in the rays.

> **When Jesus spoke again to the people, he said, "I am the light of the world. Whoever follows me will never walk in darkness, but will have the light of life."**
> **—John 8:12 (NIV)**

JOY ALL AROUND US

Winter, by Tara

Despite spending most of my years to date in the South (78 percent of my years, if you want to get technical about it), there is a part of me, deep down, that knows I am a northern girl at heart. When the little red line inside the thermometers dips below freezing, when there is a quiet echo in the brisk air, when the trees are bare and naked, a little voice inside of me whispers, "This is where you come from. This is home."

It's perhaps a bit ironic; I think people from the North are generally not winter's biggest fans. They grow tired of being pummeled by snow and ice, shoveling driveways, and spending months cooped up inside. Rushing out to buy milk and bread every time a storm is about to hit and routinely washing the salt off of cars probably gets old after a while. Perhaps the grass is (quite literally) greener on the other side, and those who have spent the majority of their years up north long to migrate south.

Maybe, one day, when I can move back to a northern state, I'll get it. I'll quickly grow tired of frozen fingertips, shivering, and scraping blocks of ice off the windshield of my car every morning. As of right now, however, I can make a solid case for the oft-overlooked season.

"Don't you think winter is so romantic?" I routinely ask those around me.

"Umm, not really. I don't know…I guess?" they routinely answer.

I think winter is incredibly romantic. Not romantic merely in the sense that it's a cozy backdrop for two people in love, but romantic in the sense of its overall charm. Winter is an idyllic setting, no matter your relationship status.

For starters, and perhaps the easiest argument to make, the winter means holidays. It means spending cherished time with loved ones, eating pumpkin pie, and seeing the excited anticipation for Christmas morning on the face of a child. The winter means crowded malls decked in tinsel and decorative gift boxes, snowflakes, and an excuse to bundle up with hot cocoa and a good book. It's peppermint bark, pumpkin-flavored *everything*, and rich food and drink.

The winter means taking a much-needed, short break from work or school after a long, tiring year. It means new beginnings, setting goals, and renewal. The winter means blankets of white snow, slushy streets, and hurrying to get to the next destination that promises an opportunity to thaw.

The winter means cozy mittens, curling up by the fireplace like a house cat, and bustling streets lined in twinkly lights. It means chunky, wooly sweaters, snow angels, and seeing your breath in the glow of the night. The winter is that jittery bounce up and down to keep warm, and the invigorating chill that makes you feel awake and alive, no caffeine necessary.

Most importantly, the winter is about giving, doing good deeds, and reminding loved ones that you care. The winter season radiates love.

I could go on for ages. I could write an entire book about winter, about every reason I personally find the popularized *Game of Thrones* expression "Winter is coming" to evoke excited anticipation rather than fearful dread. I know summer is a fan favorite, but perchance winter can be too. We just have to know where to look, and take the storms with a grain of salt. ;)

Always be joyful.
—1 Thessalonians 5:16 (NLT)

Seeing Your Child's Gifts Flourish, by Gary

Parents are often in the best position to recognize and appreciate their children's gifts. I am not referring to bikes, balls, or ballet shoes—but rather the traits, skills, bodily stature, talents, and cognitive abilities that make them particularly good at something.

Undoubtedly, the judgment of some parents is colored by their abiding love, own ambitions, or unabashed optimism.

Many times, though, parents can spot certain affinities and skills at an early age and see them evolve over time.

For instance, boys who are built with a mighty core and legs resembling a pair of oak trees just may end up being the pulling guard bludgeoning open space for their football team's star running back. The little girl who passionately sings along with the nursery school teacher or the radio is more likely to end up fronting a band, performing in her high school musical, or harmonizing in the chorus. The toddler with an affinity for solving problems might be a future *Jeopardy!* champion, engineer, or simply a sought-after mentor.

There is a special joy when you spot these gifts in your child and witness them flourish.

Often, a parent identifies the talents before their child recognizes them. It can be troubling when a gift is spotted but the child has little interest in pursuing it. Other times, a child seemingly embraces a gift shortly after standing against the coffee table for the first time and develops a lifelong passion.

My wife and I recognized ways that our daughter was blessed from an early age. Some of those gifts included writing, art, singing, kindness, and a nurturing heart.

Her sports resume was relatively short, but, fueled by the tremendous tenacity of a fighter's spirit, she enjoyed success in the one sport she chose. She obviously needed to have some tennis skills to play four years of varsity tennis on state-ranked teams and win a large percentage of her matches, but it was her heart that made the difference.

I have always been her biggest fan. That seems right, noble, and normal—but it does not escape Tara. So, unfortunately, she grades my feedback on a curve, instinctively assuming overt bias. Everything gets ratcheted down a couple notches or even discounted altogether.

Bias may be inherent in a father-daughter relationship, but I also have always had a keen eye at the plate. I can definitely call balls and strikes, but Tara would have to be convinced through her own realization rather than my encouragement.

We have been blessed to see that unfold. After graduating with honors in communications (journalism and advertising) and launching her career, Tara devotes abundant time to pursuing her passion for writing and art on the side. Thankfully, she has received enough positive feedback elsewhere to elevate my assessment credibility.

I have long been unsuccessful in convincing Tara that she possesses pitch and vocal skills. Recently, she shocked my wife and me by sending us an a cappella recording. Our first reaction was to wonder the name of the artist, but we then quickly realized it was Tara. Needless to say, I was pleased to know that my called strike on the corner was right on the mark despite her previous protests.

She has been working on writing a novel for the past year, along with freelance writing and her contributions here. She teased us with an excerpt from the book that brought tears to my eyes, as her gift for imagery and articulation was richly apparent. Her short articles entertain and educate with lighthearted humor, wisdom, and wit.

As I know other parents will attest, it has been wonderful seeing Tara embrace her special talents and nurture them to bloom. I anxiously await seeing the full, glorious bouquet that is coming.

What may be most exciting of all, though, is that perhaps her greatest gift is a humble heart.

> **Children are a gift from the Lord;**
> **they are a reward from him.**
> **—Psalm 127:3 (NLT)**

New Family Member, by Beth

As many couples do, my husband and I often have opposite tendencies. Although this can sometimes cause friction in a marriage, overall I believe it is for the best and creates a more balanced and temperate family and home.

When we lost Adidas, I knew fairly quickly that I wanted to find another cat to bring into our family. And by *quickly* I mean it was within days. I also knew it might be a bit hard to get Gary onboard with this idea.

At this time we were living in an apartment and were in the process of building our new home. While at a lighting store with my builder's designer, I was given tickets to a home show. I am not a home show enthusiast, but I took the tickets, thinking maybe it made sense as we still had a lot of decisions to make concerning our house. When I got home and looked at the home show details online, one thing quickly caught my eye. In an instant I was very excited to go to this show. As I read the details about a local rescue group bringing in animals who needed homes, I knew with certainty I had good reason to attend.

I did not tell Gary what my true agenda was concerning the home show. Thankfully he was fine with the idea of spending part of our Saturday afternoon walking through exhibits and listening to sales pitches. When we got inside the large convention center, I quickly scanned the area looking for where the shelter was set up. I wanted to make sure we didn't miss it.

I couldn't see it upon entering but continued to look as we went up and down aisles. Occasionally, in my anticipation of the real goal, I found myself easing Gary along when he got drawn into an exhibit. Finally, I saw cages. I steered us in that direction and commented about the cuteness of some of the puppies. *Ease him into looking at the cats,* I thought to myself. Sadly, we went through the entire section, and I did not find myself drawn to any of the expectant faces.

Then, in the back of the building, I saw another group of cages. As I scanned both the excited and sleepy inhabitants of all the cages, my eyes zeroed in on one skinny black kitten. I went over and read her short bio. Her name was Serena. When I saw the words "sweet, loving and good with other cats," my excitement grew. I could hardly wait to hold her.

As I picked up her skinny frame, she climbed up on my chest, and then higher as she nuzzled into my neck. It seemed she was hanging on for dear life. I guess you could say she had me at hello, and I like to think the feeling was mutual. I would have been very happy to take her home then and there, but I knew Gary needed more time to get used to the idea.

As we drove home, I was purposeful to talk about her and her attributes. The next day I did the same. Quickly I advanced the idea of inquiring if Serena had been adopted at the show. When Gary said he was okay with this idea, I knew it was all over but the shouting—that is, unless she had already found a home.

I sent out an e-mail inquiring about Serena, saying a prayer that she hadn't been adopted. Thankfully the response back was an answer to my prayer: she was still available. With Gary away on business and an empty crate in the passenger seat, I headed to a nearby town to get our newest furry blessing.

As I headed home with Serena in a crate next to me, I didn't know all that adding her to our family would entail, but I was most definitely filled with joy.

> **Weeping may last through the night,
> but joy comes with the morning.
> —Psalm 30:5 (NLT)**

Singing in Your Car Like a Rock Star, by Gary

For some reason, often the best place to enjoy your favorite tunes is while driving alone in your car. This is especially true when you want to crank it up and belt out the song like a rock star.

Feeling like you are hermetically sealed in a moving sound chamber with no one else but a passing driver to witness us can bring out our best inner rock star. No inhibitions or fear of missing that note—or maybe more accurately, notes.

And if you are like me, you don't even have to worry about being corrected by your spouse when you butcher the lyrics. (That "Pour Some Sugar on Me" commercial rings all too true for me.)

The vehicular speed and motion only serve to enhance the musical experience. Perhaps you mix in a little drumming on the dash or even some momentary one-handed air guitar.

It could be the next best thing to being center stage—at least until you reach your destination. Depending on where you were going, the full-blown rock concert might suddenly morph into humming, whistling, or background vocals.

Surely, solo performances flow most readily with the absence of stage fright, but the rolling sound studio is not off limits to collaboration. Many a long-distance journey might have bordered on agony without a joint passenger concert performance belting out some Bon Jovi songs, "American Pie," and other all-time classics.

Similarly, what would cruising the boulevard or your equivalent local main drag be without blasting out some loud tunes? And weren't those drives home even sweeter with some good group vocalizing while basking in the afterglow of a big team victory? Would the excitement of heading out on vacation be anywhere near as joyful without a good sing-along on the drive?

Regardless of the occasion, is there any doubt about the joy we experience when we are rolling along the highway doing our best impressions of Maroon 5, Foreigner, Casting Crowns, or Carrie Underwood?

> **Shout for joy to the Lord, all the earth,**
> **burst into jubilant song with music.**
> **—Psalm 98:4 (NIV)**

CHAPTER 11
Joy in Many Places

Gratitude, by Beth

When our daughter, Tara, was in grade school, we started a family journal that we filled out at the end of the day, usually prior to Tara going to bed. We each noted the best thing that happened to us during the day (our high), the worst thing that happened to us during the day (our low), and three things for which we were thankful. These were listed as our blessings for that day.

At the time I thought this practice would be a good way to keep the lines of communication open with Tara. Daily we would be informed about what she was excited about as well as things that were causing her worry, fear, or sadness. I also believed teaching her to be aware of and thankful for her blessings was an important attitude for her to cultivate in her heart.

Recently as I was cleaning my office, I came across our old journals. Reading through our entries was a way to journey back into that season of our lives. Often the entries for our highs of the day as well as our blessings involved spending time with friends or family. Everyday-type blessings like a good grade on a test or a day off from work were also common. Looking back over our lows reminded me that most of the daily irritants we face are just a blip on the radar screen of our lives. In a month, or a week, sometimes even as quickly as within the hour, they will be forgotten. As I packed the journals away and continued on my quest for a more organized office, I realized the overall feeling produced from reading our journals was gratitude. The goal sought in writing the journals was realized, once again, in their reading.

A few years ago, I started the practice of mentally listing twenty-five things I am thankful for as I wait to fall asleep each night. I must admit most nights my day has been full and I am tired as I climb into bed, so almost every day my first mental entry is my thankfulness for being in bed! And in the spirit of full disclosure, on nights when I am even more tired, I'm sure I fall asleep before I complete my list. Perhaps it is my version of counting sheep.

In all seriousness, however, it is much more than an aid to falling asleep. It is my way of going to my provider, my Father, the Lord, and thanking Him for His goodness and His faithfulness to me. How easy it is to go through our days and miss the many small ways we are blessed. I don't believe in luck or karma, but instead stand on James 1:17. Nightly I remind myself of the many things I have to be thankful for and who deserves that thanks.

> **Every good and perfect gift is from above, coming down from the Father of the heavenly lights, who does not change like shifting shadows.**
> **—James 1:17 (NIV)**

Visiting Your Favorite Vacation Spot, by Gary

There is always a feeling of joyful anticipation that builds inside of me as we drive toward this small island at the Jersey Shore. This phenomenon goes as far back as my memory will reach, as my family has a deep connection with this unique city at the southern end of the state.

My family temporarily lived here when I was an infant, before relocating a couple hours away to a small town in southeastern Pennsylvania. My mother grew up in this resort town, where my grandparents and her sister's family remained. This, of course, offered many opportunities to visit and vacation.

A well-known national publication has consistently rated Ocean City, New Jersey, as the number-one family resort in the country. And for good reason—small kids to senior citizens will attest to this lofty rating.

Four bridges connect the island to the mainland. It seems fittingly emblematic that Ocean City is officially separated by water all around, as crossing one of those four bridges transports you to a tremendously unique and special atmosphere.

Century-old blue laws still prevail, mandating hours of business operation and maintaining the municipality as a dry town. Despite the absence of adult beverages, Ocean City offers a little bit of everything to appeal across the full spectrum of the population.

The oceanfront and bay offer typical fun in the sun, including lounging on the beach, swimming, water sports, and beach volleyball. A quaint downtown remains with little shops and restaurants. Single- and multifamily homes line the streets and are well maintained with the colorful, pride-of-ownership landscaping of yesteryear throughout the island.

The largest attraction, which serves to meld everyone from young to old, is the boardwalk. Bikes and joggers predominate in the mornings, yielding to foot traffic the remainder of the day, with benches lining the entire expanse for those who just want to peacefully observe. A two-mile stretch presents an amazing array of options, from shopping to food to amusement rides to water slides to movie theaters to miniature golf to aspiring musical performers to special events at the music pier.

Did I mention food? Besides a range of restaurant options, the Ocean City boardwalk offers the simple pleasures of the very best junk food on earth. As you can read in a separate essay entitled "Pizza," this includes the best pizza on the planet, ice cream, frozen custard, water ice, soft pretzels, cotton candy, homemade fudge, saltwater taffy, fresh popcorn, and just about anything your culinary desires can conjure up.

From May to September, the boardwalk is surely *the* place to hang out. A wave of humanity courses up and down these wooden boards raised fifteen feet above and running parallel to the sandy, oceanfront beaches. The moonlight, cool ocean breeze, and rhythmic ebb and flow of waves provide additional ambience in the evenings. Although the atmosphere appeals to all, the boardwalk experience for teenagers might be a little bit of heaven on earth.

My love for this small town that grows twenty-fold in population during the summer extends further. It is laced with great memories of spending time with our extended family, including sharing the joy of this special place with my wife and daughter, as my parents once did with me. How blessed have I been to combine those gatherings and memories with a truly special place perhaps unlike any other in this world?

I feel joy the moment my feet hit this little island in New Jersey. Most of you likely have a similar favorite vacation spot that evokes great memories and emotions. Where is your Ocean City?

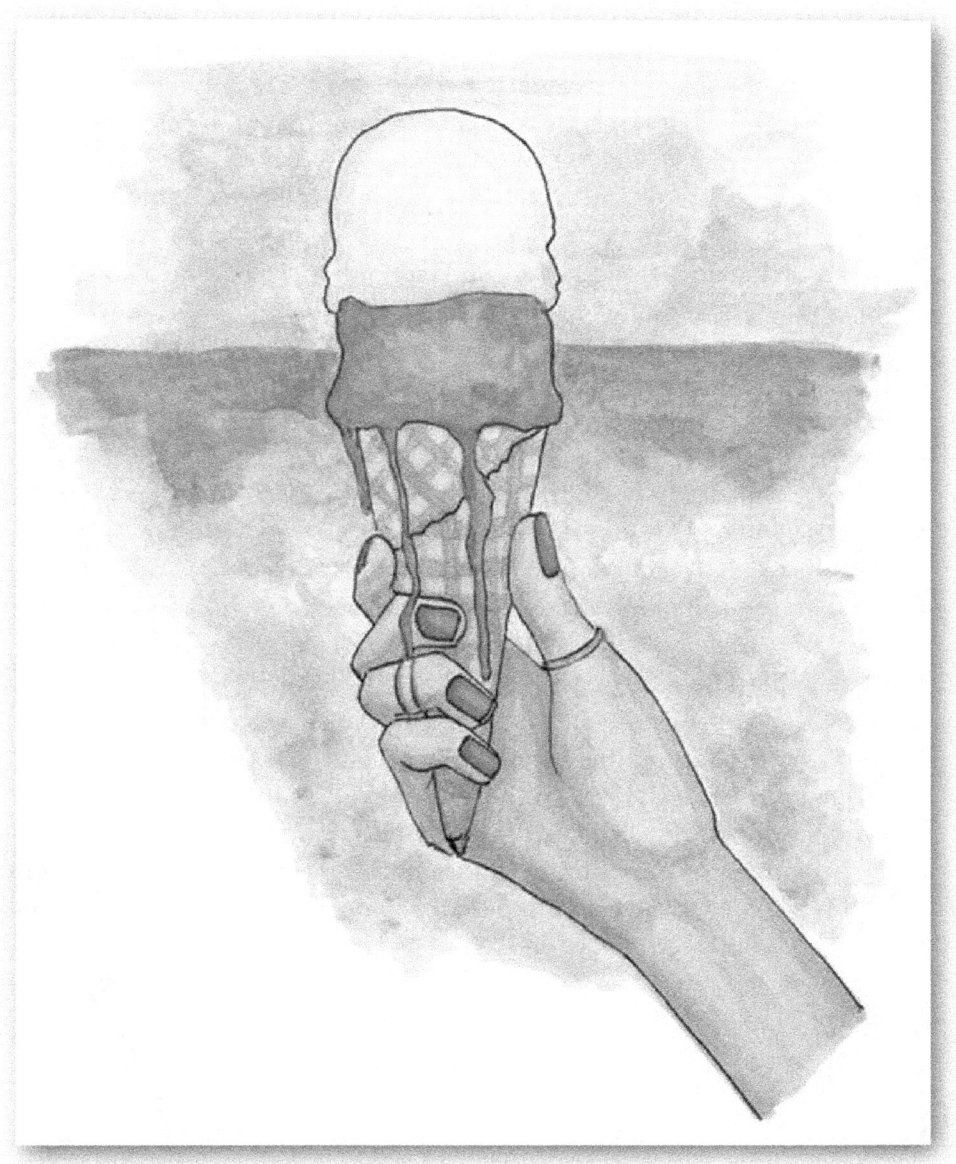

Sunrises and Early Starts, by Gary

Full disclosure—I am not an early riser by nature. Despite having had a lengthy career in the corporate world, full of early-morning meetings and travel schedules, early starts to the day do not come naturally to me.

Through the years, I have always suspected that my biological clock might migrate in that direction, but that has not been the case. After all, my father was usually working on his second cup of coffee by sunrise. My father-in-law arose even earlier, anxious to see what splendor the new day would hold.

My calculus-driven mind kept suggesting that this habit would evolve as the pages of the calendar turned.

The C-suite executives almost flaunted it as an act of discipline, seeming to compete to see who could call the earliest meetings. This demanded an early ring of my alarm clock but never evoked a change in personal preference.

Surely, part of the reason that I am not an early bird is that I remain tenaciously intent on squeezing every last ounce out of the previous day. When you are still catching up on e-mail, reading, or simply doing some of the things you couldn't squeeze into the day's prime hours subsequent to the date advancing on your iPhone, your body tends to crave just a few more z's in the morning.

Despite the settings on my internal clock and my innate tendencies, I find it highly interesting that when I do arise early, I feel energized. This is especially true when the sun has not yet peeked over the horizon.

There is something calm and peaceful about watching the light bloom in the eastern sky at dawn that is almost inherently spiritual. Light is goodness. Time seems to slow down, perhaps by God's design, providing the perfect opportunity to reflect on and marvel at the new day.

A sense of gratitude and appreciation rushes over me for every day that has passed and the new day that is about to unfold.

The experience highlights my smallness in the grand cosmic scheme of things and the wonder of God's universe. This emotion is not one of emptiness or insignificance, but rather one of joy. It is as if God has the world in the palm of His hand and has it all covered for us.

He created this unbelievably intricate, impossibly complex, and perfectly calibrated order, which exceeds even the most intelligent human minds' comprehension. He knows what was, what is, and what is to come.

Watching the rays of brilliant sunlight gently stream over the eastern sky at dawn, as dependable as the laws of gravity, serves to underscore God's perfect order and awesome power. As I take it all in, a feeling of joy almost invariably wells up inside of me, almost in direct synchronization with the sunrise.

Because of the impact on me and the way it touches my inner being, perhaps there is still hope for me to become an early riser.

> **The whole earth is filled with awe at your wonders; where morning dawns, where evening fades, you call forth songs of joy.**
> **—Psalm 65:8 (NIV)**

Telecommunications, by Gary

Most of those who have been welcomed into our world subsequent to the Generation X segment likely do not comprehend or appreciate how cellular technology has drastically changed our lives. For those of us on the other side of this demarcation line, we might even see the evolution of telecom as somewhat of a modern miracle.

Technological advancement continues to render separation of time and space meaningless in terms of personal communication. We can now pretty much communicate with anybody, anytime, anyplace. Applications like FaceTime and Skype bring us even closer than a spoken or written word, heightening the perils of bad hair days and lounging in your underwear along the way.

Immediacy is upon us.

Besides being able to virtually connect with anyone in an instant, information about anything that might cross your mind is just a few keystrokes or verbal commands away. As its name promises, Instagram, as well as the more "old school" Facebook and LinkedIn social media outlets, provides updates timely and frequently. You no longer have to wonder what Nikki or Jason is doing—you get a notification that their smiling mugs are awaiting a download on your phone. Connectivity also comes replete with risqué content, déjà vu selfies, and endless videos from a broad swath of people you do not currently—nor aspire to—know.

Reaching back a few decades into the archives of human history, we found a much less communicative and connected world. Of course, this can have its downside for sure, but we now enjoy tremendous enhancements in convenience, information, and communication. And cellular technology now is the conduit or enabler for much of our personal entertainment.

Telephone booths once dotted the inhabited landscape, but they are now mostly artifacts found in museums, or perhaps they're used to add ambience and authenticity outside your favorite trendy English pub. By the 1990s, these little glass boxes with folding doors and Humvee-esque steel phones began going the way of the dinosaur population. Modern evolution also spawned the less claustrophobic wall-mounted, glass-encased armored pay phone.

JOY ALL AROUND US

As a bit of educational fodder, although somewhat unimaginable to younger readers, we are only a few decades removed from the need to search for one of these artifacts to communicate on the go. They were "pay as you go" and "long-distance charges apply" all the way—forget it if you didn't have a dime on you. Telephones were hardwired in our homes, progressing from rotary dials to touch-tone and corded to wireless.

The previous household-to-household phone connection has now been replaced by person-to-person multifaceted communication. The implications of this are farther reaching than what our daughter might understand. For instance, it required some courage to call that girl you had your eye on in junior high, as the odds were that her parents, or even worse, a smart-alecky and judgmental older sibling, might answer. The direct and less intimidating option of texting Sherri was not an option. And the parents always sounded sternly unamused rather than like an inebriated trombone with a muffle like in those Charlie Brown cartoons.

Speaking of phones, even that expression is archaic. The telephone has morphed into PDAs, smartphones, and the tragically named phablets. Sometimes a mulligan is in order, but regardless of the nomenclature, the point is that phones now serve multiple functions besides audio communication. Did I mention texting?

Cellular technology itself has changed dramatically since its inception. The first-generation mobile phone was somewhat equivalent to installing a home phone in your vehicle. This was replaced by the infamous bag phone, which essentially required you to lug a seventeen-pound piece of luggage around. This advanced to the comical Kleenex-box-sized handset with a fourteen-inch antenna. Think Gordon Gekko in the 1987 hit movie *Wall Street*. From there, they got progressively smaller and "flippier" before rebounding to the current standard flat screen that seems to expand with every new release. I respectfully refer to this period in cellular history as the Can You Hear Me Now Era.

Today, when we pick up a smartphone, we hold in our hands a multifunction communication device and entertainment bundle all in one.

We can make a reservation in minutes or get directions from our car. We can easily communicate vocally or textually with multiple people in a variety of locations in real time. We can stare each other in the eye while conversing despite being hundreds of miles apart. Breaking news or the answer to any question is available in seconds.

In addition, entertainment options abound. We can stream and download videos or even full-length movies to watch at our convenience. Our entire music library, equivalent to seven hundred pounds of vinyl records, can reside on our device to enjoy with earbuds or a wireless speaker. Fantasy football live scoring updates are in the palms of our hands, unless of course you are at a football game where the thirty-seven thousand other fans checking their teams are killing the bandwidth. Virtually the entire world's library of books and periodicals is now available in digital format to read on your smartphone.

Besides the tremendous advancement in convenience, modern cellular technology enables many hours of enjoyment. This is a far cry from its ancestral audio-only device wired to the wall.

Heart of God, by Beth

It is not unusual for me to cry in church; to be honest I cry almost every week. No one around me notices except maybe my husband, who may see a few tears running down my cheek or notice my hurried search for a tissue. Sometimes I shed a few tears during worship as I feel the Spirit of God in the room and the lyrics of the music touch my heart. More often it is during the sermon as the pastor's words speak to me in a personal way.

On this day I started crying after the service was over, as I was exiting the sanctuary. Not only was the timing unusual, but this was not just a few tears—this was me fighting back the tears as I walked to our car. My husband noticed and asked me what was wrong. I told him I would explain later. Once I was safely in our car, I could not hold back any longer—the tears came, and loudly.

How do I explain? I think by saying that for a brief time, and in a small way, I was feeling the heart of God. I wish I could say this happens to me a lot, but the truth is, as most people, I am more often self-centered and oblivious to the hurts around me. Or sometimes, feeling overwhelmed by the sadness and pains people face around the world, I find it easier to shut down and distract myself from feeling their pain.

Today I couldn't shut down. I could start crying right now if I would let myself go back to the scene. You might be surprised by what brought on my tears—not a sad sight, but a beautiful one. It was a pair of bright, beautiful, and full-of-life eyes. I watched them as I was making my way up the aisle. I watched as they looked up at the people walking by them. If eyes can smile, and we all know they can, these eyes were doing just that. They seemed to be trying to reach out with love to all who were passing by. As I observed this, I noticed that I seemed to be the only one who saw these beautiful eyes trying to connect with someone. I was determined to strike up a conversation or at least say hello when I reached them. The more I watched, the more my heart was broken. When I finally reached the lady these eyes belonged to, someone stepped between us, and my opportunity began to slip away. Then the woman who was pushing her wheelchair turned her around and ushered her out of the area. I never did connect with the eyes that moved my heart of compassion.

Where does one go after that? God had a purpose to allow me to feel His pain that profoundly.

Maybe God wanted to remind me to be more aware of the people around me, the people I see in my daily life: family, friends, and even strangers. Daily, I need to ask God to help me remain open to the needs of those around me, and how I might, in some small way, be able to meet them. If I can grow in this area, I will not only find myself doing His will more often, but I will also open myself up to being able to feel the heart of God. I don't imagine there could be a more joy-filled place to be.

Retreats to the Wilderness, by Tara

I'm a city girl by heart—anyone who knows me can tell you that much. I love the smoggy breeze, the bustling streets, and the feeling that you could simply slip into the crowd and disappear. I love the air of excitement, the bright, twinkly lights, and the cocktail lullaby of horns, sirens, and traffic. I love that a city allows you to be both totally alone and coexist with thousands of others at the exact same time.

I love the freedom of individuality in cities. I love how you don't have to be anyone in particular when you live in a sprawling metropolis. You can be someone new every day, if you'd like. Nobody even has to know your name.

"If you're going to live in the city, do it while you're young and single," many have advised.

I can't object to that counsel. While you're young, living in a city allows you to find yourself—really, *really* find yourself at the very core of your existence. The city allows you to uncover the layers of pretenses, masquerades, and makeup that you piled on in your formative years when you felt there was a specific type of person you were *supposed* to be, when you felt you needed to put on a show.

But then, you're expected to retreat to suburbia after your city years, after you "get it out of your system." You're expected to settle down and raise a family in a nice, green cul-de-sac where your children will graduate from strollers to training wheels to bicycles, all within the same neighborhood block. Your children are supposed to grow up the same way you did—under the pretenses, masquerades, and makeup, because suburbia breeds such.

This is where I disagree. I hope to raise my children in the city. I want them to know diversity, individuality, and tolerance. I think cities nurture wisdom, develop character, and encourage independence. I can't think of a better environment for both myself and my future family.

But, all that said, there's a special place in my heart for the wilderness. Specifically, the mountains.

The mountains are the only place outside of city limits where I can go and rethink everything I so firmly believe, just for a moment.

Maybe I should live out here, I think to myself as I breathe in the fresh, pine-needly air.

And then I devise an entirely new life plan.

I would move into a quiet mountain home with a gravel driveway and a small black bear figurine on the front steps. The house would be constructed of ochre- or sienna-colored logs and overlook the ever-changing foliage in the back. There would be one or two nice neighbors down the hill to get together with every once in a while and talk about the weather.

My daily routine would boast minimal stress. I would wake up in the mornings, brew a pot of coffee, and settle in with a good book on the rocker on the back porch. I'd pen novels, paint with vivid watercolors, and take crisp photos—a different activity every day, all inspired by the beautiful quiet.

There would be isolation, and that would be okay. My uniform would be flannel shirts and cozy knit socks; I'd never pay a second thought to my messy hair. Quality family time would be guaranteed, not on an "as work permits" basis. I would pick wild blackberries in the backyard with my children and snuggle up by the fireplace with my husband on late nights in the dead of winter.

It would be a sweet, simple existence, this fictional home in the mountains. But that's all it is—fiction.

I'm a city girl, after all. The city is and always will be my reality, and that's okay. It makes retreats to the wilderness all the sweeter. They're visits that I can relish and cherish, a temporary haven so special that it makes time extend, the clock tick more slowly.

> **The grasslands of the wilderness overflow;**
> **the hills are clothed with gladness.**
> **—Psalm 65:12 (NIV)**

JOY ALL AROUND US

The Next Best Thing, by Gary

Sometimes circumstances make your first choice infeasible or simply not an option. Perhaps sticker shock on the vehicle you had your eye on led you to a more sensible purchase. If possible, a good alternative is to go to the next best thing.

When a sore shoulder, distant travel, and a business career made continuing a baseball career less feasible, I was fortunate to have a good alternative. Fast-pitch softball became the next best thing for me.

Taking the fundamental game-within-a-game pitcher-batter confrontation out of the equation made slow-pitch softball unappealing. Conversely, despite the oversized ball and the shrunken dimensions, fast-pitch softball most closely mirrored baseball. Additionally, the smaller fields facilitated playing in the evening under lights, which eliminated the need to make an early break from the office.

The pitcher-versus-batter showdown was every bit as intense in fast-pitch softball. Similarly, pitchers still desired to blow fastballs past hitters and mix in deceptive movements and changes of speed. All baseball-honed skills were transferrable. And by the way, as my body will attest, there is nothing soft about the ball or the sport.

Although baseball first grabbed my heart and turned into a twenty-year-long affection, softball eased the pain of the breakup. In fact, it offered so much more than just a soft landing. Although I tend to meld these two close-as-cousins sports together, my gradual transition into softball really spawned a second career of similar duration.

In reality, the softball experience surpassed baseball in terms of excitement and joy for many reasons. Although I was blessed with some great moments in baseball, most were more personal in nature. Conversely, softball was filled with team accomplishments and an interpersonal bond with other players.

While baseball was marked by constant teammate turnover and change, softball offered an enduring stability. Although there was surely the natural ebb and flow of players coming and going, our teams revolved around a core nucleus that stuck together for most, if not all, of two decades. We achieved sporting success together, but more importantly, we developed a deep bond and friendship.

Surely, a big part of this bond derived from climbing the mountains of accomplishment together. We are blessed to have shared many great achievements, including championships at the local, state, and regional levels. Although we never quite pulled off a national championship, we also had the great fortune of competing for one on a handful of occasions.

Those days on the field surely yielded many joyous moments, from late-game rallies to hard-fought victories to trophy presentations. Jubilant screams, abundant high fives, animated backslaps, and raucous, spontaneous celebrations were all part of the experience, but perhaps the most rewarding aspects were less tangible.

There is something truly special about working together to achieve team goals. Some talent helps, but it also requires perseverance, tenacity, courage, confidence, individual contribution, the will to win, and an unwavering belief in each other.

And no matter what, we always had fun. Laughter was a constant in the calculus, both during the heat of battle and just hanging out together. Although the journey of life has now placed us on different paths, the times we do get together are punctuated with smiles and laughter as we replay the memories and remind ourselves why we bonded like brothers.

Along the way, like any team, we suffered humility and disappointment. For our group, though, victory or defeat, adversity or good fortune, we embraced the fun, laughter, and joy! Little did we know at the time, we were modeling a recipe for happiness in the broader stage of life.

We all face choices and limitations in our journey through life. Our resilience in responding to those situations can have a profound impact on our happiness. Finding and embracing the next best thing has the power to transform disappointment into joy. Is there a next best thing awaiting you?

Trees, by Gary

The expression "can't see the forest for the trees" is one that I have invoked on many occasions throughout my life. This saying has always resonated with me, as it is an apt metaphor for a circumstance that very frequently occurs. I have surely encountered it countless times throughout my business career, but this myopia can pervade anywhere in life.

Sometimes it relates to problem solving, where individuals get so bogged down in ideas and information that they are unable to find the solution. Other times, it speaks to becoming so engrossed with the detail that the objectives or outcomes drop from sight. Or it is simply a matter of focusing on the individual brush strokes and failing to see the big picture.

Typically, the resolution comes from stepping back and broadening your view.

Overall, it has served me well in leadership roles to be blessed with a natural inclination to focus on the big picture. Staying focused on the desired outcomes and what it will take to achieve them ultimately defines success. It is worth noting, though, that without those blessed with the ability to concentrate on the parts (or trees), few objectives would be achieved.

Recently, as I reflected on the natural world created by God, I stumbled on an interesting personal paradox. Ironically, when it comes to trees, it would be safe to say that I have not been able to see the forest for the trees.

Sadly, my tendency has been to largely take them for granted. One could argue the opposite—that I was, in fact, seeing only the forest and looking past the trees. But my recent realization was that I only saw the tree itself and failed to see all the things that make it so much more than a wooden trunk with leaves.

The leaves and flowers brighten our world with rich colors as they grow and bloom. Somewhat incredibly, most also provide an even more spectacular display during autumn's withering, turning electric shades of yellow, orange, and red.

These tall, bark-covered spires bear fruit and nuts, some of the most nutritious and delicious foods we know. They have literally provided the building blocks of shelter for centuries.

Scientifically, trees convert carbon dioxide into oxygen. Simply put, they transform poison into the very substance that our bodies need to function. At the most fundamental level, they represent life!

In so many ways, trees are a marvelous wonder and God's grand work of art. From their humble seedling beginnings, they first plant firmly beneath the surface before rising up from the ground and growing ever taller for many, many years to come. Each stands as a triumph of nature, many towering majestically toward the sky.

It is no wonder that trees are often the objects of biblical imagery and metaphor. They are towers of strength. They are more than what we see at a glance, as they are rooted in an invisible, intricate foundation of extraordinary strength. They provide sustenance. They symbolize our ancestral lineage. They demonstrate perseverance and stand the test of time. They connote a covenant. Plain and simple—trees are life.

Similarly, perhaps it is also no wonder that I recently developed an otherwise unexplainable fascination with the oak tree across the street from our home. Multiple times, I have been compelled to scurry outside to photograph this magnificent oak tree in different lights and atmospheric conditions. Other times, I find my eyes drawn its way and my gaze fixed on it for several minutes as I admire its strength and splendor. My photo collection is now pushing toward triple digits, but it is clear that there are more photo shoots of this subject to come.

On closer examination, this majestic pillar of strength is actually two trees side by side, perfectly complementing each other to present as one to casual observers. This peculiarity only serves to enhance my fascination and the grand old oak's appeal.

Although they went underappreciated much of my life, I now can see the forest for the trees when it comes to trees. In fact, keeping a watchful eye on this one particular oak across the street evokes a bit of joy.

> **Let the fields and their crops burst out with joy! Let the trees of the forest sing for joy.**
> **—Psalm 96:12 (NLT)**

CHAPTER 12
Natural Joys

Plants, by Beth

As long as I can remember, I have loved having flowers and plants brightening my living spaces, both inside and out. As a young girl, I had a few houseplants that I kept in my room, my first experience with caring for something totally on my own. Outside, my parents had many different types of flowers growing in lightly tended gardens. Occasionally we would pick some blooms to enjoy their beauty inside our home. I also had a small garden of my very own. Every year I would plant the same seeds (morning glory) in this designated space, which was complete with a trellis for climbing. Once this vine is established, the flowers open in the morning and close by end of day, only to repeat this same cycle day after day. As a child, I was fascinated by this process, and I was captivated by the simple beauty of these flowers.

As an adult and homeowner, I have considerably more available space to fill with plants and flowers. Having space to fill with living beauty is a blessing, but for me it is not without its challenges. Although I love gardening, I would not say I have a green thumb—perhaps a green nail would be more accurate. In addition, I have never taken the time to acquire any real knowledge on the subject of landscaping, gardening, or even houseplants. For me it usually amounts to buying what I like and hoping for the best.

One thing that I believe offsets my lack of innate gardening acumen is the fact that I talk to my plants. My conversation consists of compliments on their beauty and encouragement on their growth. I am not deterred in the least by the fact that within these conversations, I receive very little response from my plants. Although my plants may be light on words, they respond in kind by being healthy and vibrant more often than not. This routine, I believe, has more than offset my lack of a truly green thumb.

The beauty of household greenery, garden shrubs, and flowers contributes to more joy in my day-to-day life. Beauty, both inside and outside our home, brightens my days, as I receive immediate shots of joy when I look in the direction of a blooming shrub, a newly blossomed flower, or a thriving houseplant.

> **Yes, there will be an abundance of flowers and singing and joy!**
> —Isaiah **35:2 (NLT)**

True Friends, by Gary

The people in our lives fall into a number of different categories. In some cases, they may not fall into just one but rather two or even multiple categories.

These categories tend to fall on somewhat of a continuum of familiarity and closeness. There are strangers on one end—or perhaps those whom we do not even know exist, let alone who cross paths with us. Other categories on the spectrum include acquaintances, friends, associates, and family members.

People in our lives can move through a progression across the continuum. Strangers become acquaintances who later become friends. Associates become friends. Friends may become family members. Sometimes family members would also be aptly classified as friends, which places them in two categories.

Although some personality types might differ, growing the friend bucket in your life tends to be a good thing. It helps to keep your social calendar full, ensure against loneliness, and open opportunities for fun.

In regard to friends, though, we have all experienced that not all are created equal. This does not speak to a caste system, socioeconomic standing, level of success, etc., but rather to their levels of bonding, commitment, dependability, and genuineness.

It's surely good to have friends—but it's great to have *true friends*!

True friends are there for you when you fall down or need support. They have your back when you need it most.

True friends can be trusted. You can confide in them with confidence, knowing they won't breach it. This, of course, means that your conversations tend to be more genuine and heartfelt rather than guarded.

You never have to worry if a true friend is talking behind your back. In fact, you believe they would stick up for you when others trip down the path of gossiping about you.

True friends are happy for you when you achieve success or good things come your way. They are not jealous or covetous. Heck, they might even send you a congratulatory note or join you to celebrate.

True friends encourage you and lift you up. They are not the insecure souls who wrap their underlying feelings or desires to diminish you in a cloak of jest as they poke fun at you.

True friends might speak to you in love with some heart-to-heart feedback, but they do not tear you down with attacks and hurtful words.

None of us is perfect, to say the least, so even true friends may falter and disappoint us at times. But, even so, we can typically differentiate how those in our circle of friends fall onto either side of the ledger. Our own hearts sense what is in others' hearts.

Who are you going to reach out to when you are having difficulties? Who gives you comfort when you share sensitive or intimate matters? Who is likely to speak life into you with a word of encouragement or sound advice? Whom can you count on?

Sometimes the dividing line is very fine, but your gut can almost always perceive it. Clearly not all, or even many, make the cut.

Sadly, true friends can be hard to come by, but when you find them, they are a true joy!

> **Oh, the joys of those who do not follow the advice of the wicked, or stand around with sinners, or join in with mockers.**
> **—Psalm 1:1 (NLT)**

> **Walking with a friend in the dark is better than walking alone in the light.**
> **—Helen Keller**

> **A real friend is one who walks in when the rest of the world walks out.**
> **—Walter Winchell**

The Joy of Routine and Structure, by Beth

My husband often reminds me that I am a creature of habit. He is very aware of how I navigate through my days, and he understands the importance of routines and schedules in my daily life. As our character traits are often seen more clearly by others, I had to think on this label and description before I could embrace it. To me being a creature of habit sounds boring, stuffy—and perhaps, dare I say, old. It definitely sounds like someone who is not much fun to be around. Being labeled spontaneous or free spirited, on the other hand, sounds enviable. These descriptive words make us think of one who is the life of the party, someone we would gravitate toward because they lead an exciting life. Although we can work to improve and stretch ourselves, most likely our natural bents will prevail. For me, this means lists, planning, and routines will most likely always remain a big part of my days and my life.

As I reflected on my tendencies, however, I realized there are many blessings to be found in a lifestyle that includes at least some amount of schedule and routine. I currently work from home as a writer, as well as carry the responsibility of running our household. Working from home is easy for someone like me who prefers to have daily, and even weekly, tasks planned out. I believe that if I had a more spontaneous bent, I could easily get sidetracked and find myself pursuing social activities that suddenly arise, or succumbing to the temptation of a long afternoon walk on a sunny day.

In actuality, my planning and reliance on routine permit me to be both more productive and more spontaneous. My scheduling allows me to get things accomplished in a timely manner, which provides me with pockets of time that I can fill with enjoyable activities. Because I know what I need to get accomplished every day, boundaries are easily defined. When my list is complete, I can step away and call it a day. These remaining unstructured hours can then be used to exercise my spontaneous side.

More importantly, I know that we are all created in God's image and yet completely unique. He has gifted each of us very purposefully so we are equipped for the work He has called us to do. Trying to better ourselves is always a noble pursuit, but often it makes sense to build on our natural tendencies rather than try to give oneself a personality overhaul. I am not meant to lament how I was created, but to embrace my natural tendencies with joy. And when my schedule is clear on a sunny afternoon, I plan to call one of my spontaneous friends.

> **"For I know the plans I have for you," declares the Lord, "plans to prosper you and not to harm you, plans to give you hope and a future."**
> —Jeremiah **29:11 (NIV)**

Joy in Unexpected Places, by Beth

A few days ago, I decided to go through old e-mails and delete those I no longer needed. One reason the timing was good for this endeavor was that we had recently sold our previous house after having it on the market for two years. I was looking forward to deleting the numerous pieces of correspondence with our realtor as well as builder correspondence from when we built the home only months prior to our decision to sell. It has been a whirlwind for the past three years, including multiple moves for our family and job changes for my husband. Deleting these e-mails was very cathartic; I could officially close this chapter of our life.

I had another reason for wanting to get my e-mails under control: the book you are now holding. Our family was about three weeks into our commitment to write this book, and I had been put in charge of organizing our essays. It seemed like a perfect time to clear out the old, unnecessary e-mails and make way for this new undertaking. I could hear the scripture in my head: "See, I am doing a new thing! Now it springs up; do you not perceive it?" (Isaiah 43:19 NIV).

At some point in this process, I reached the very first e-mail stored on my phone, and I noticed it was from my sister Debbie. After seeing the date and a few words in the body of the e-mail, I realized it detailed the last moments of my mother's life. I decided to print the e-mail so I could put it in a folder with other correspondence and memorial-service notes I had saved from this time.

My mother died in June of 2012. She was a widow, as we had lost my dad almost five years earlier. She was eighty-nine years old with limited vision and mobility, although her mind remained strong. In June, a broken leg resulting from a fall was enough for God to call her home rather quickly. Thankfully we arranged a conference call the day before she left this earth. Her four children, their spouses, and her grandchildren were on the call to send her off with love and thankfulness for her life. She had not been coherent very much since her fall earlier in the week, only occasionally responding to a caregiver or family member visiting her. My sister and brother, who were with her in person, were convinced that even with eyes closed, her mumbling and nodding proved she was tracking every word spoken to her during our call.

When I sat down to read the e-mail from my sister, I only got as far as the first sentence. "A nurse named Joy was with Mom when she took her last breath and she told me Mom died peacefully." I call moments that speak to me like this "God hugs." Here we were only just beginning our journey with creating a book about joy, when God wanted to remind me of who was with my mother when she went to be with Him. Joy comes in many forms and is found in many places. Here I found it wrapped in the sadness of the loss of my mother. This time it was a reminder that God gets involved in the big details as well as the small, and it was wrapped up with a bow named Joy.

Hands, by Tara

When I was a girl of single digits, my father and I would study our hands. We'd hold our hands up under the light, and we'd study every knuckle, every line, every crease, every bony bump, and every tip of every finger.

We did this because we had noticed that we had the same hands.

My dad would exclaim, "Your hands are a carbon copy of mine!"

It was true. Just smaller, and perhaps a bit daintier.

Looking back on it now, it would seem more plausible to think that this was just a sweet thing my father said to me as a kid to make me feel special. Along the lines of the existence of a jolly old man who delivers gifts to children across the globe, it's a well-intentioned piece of fiction. For instance, the parent who allows his or her child to win at cards, checkers, or basketball means no malice by being dishonest. It's a loving gesture that promotes feelings of confidence and self-worth.

It's not too far-fetched to think that a loving parent would make a little show about how much their child looks like them, because the child is a part of them, after all, and they share a special bond because of this. But I don't think this was the case with my father's and my hands.

Besides evidence of sharing DNA, I think having my father's hands is an earthly, tangible reminder that we are made in our Father's image. It was no mistake, no hoax. We are wonderfully and fearfully made, and God gave me my father's hands. He gave me my father's hands not only so I could be reminded of my earthly father, but so we could both be reminded of our Heavenly Father too.

> **So God created mankind in his own image,**
> **in the image of God he created them;**
> **male and female he created them.**
> **—Genesis 1:27 (NIV)**

Forgiveness, by Gary

As figurative card-carrying members of the human race, we are all subject to doing stupid things. No matter how robust we believe our moral compass might be, all of us err in our ways. Mistakes are what we do.

The Free Dictionary defines the adjective *human* this way: "Subject to or indicative of the weaknesses, imperfections, and fragility associated with humans."

By our very nature, we say inappropriate things, hurt others' feelings, engage in selfish acts, fail to act to support someone in need, exhibit a prideful heart, or commit a variety of other transgressions. No need to pound this one into the turf—you get the idea because you have been on both sides of the transaction countless times.

Sometimes, the matter is just between God and us. Other times, we may have offended one or multiple others in our actions or inactions.

In either case, being forgiven lifts the burden that rests on our souls, whether the transgression is large or small or somewhere in between. Getting right with the offended party by admitting your mistake, apologizing, and hearing "no worries" or "I forgive you" in response provides great relief.

In the end, if you are truly remorseful, forgiveness delivers a tremendous sense of joy.

Without question, Jesus provided the ultimate deliverance by dying for our sins. Is there any better reason to rejoice than knowing as a believer that God has already forgiven us?

Similarly, He wants us to offer that same grace to others, no matter how badly we feel harmed or offended. That can seem almost impossible at times, particularly in the heat of the moment, but it becomes much easier when you consider that this is exactly what He does with each of us day after day.

It is also important to recognize the positive impact forgiveness has on the offending party. If that person is sincerely remorseful, forgiveness turns their distress into joy and allows both sides to move on. Besides, who couldn't use a do-over or mulligan now and then?

God makes it abundantly clear that these emotions are just as wrong, but really—is there any joy in holding on to bitterness, anger, resentment, or a vengeful heart? Negative emotions are like toxins eating away at your inner core whether you consciously recognize it or not.

And admit it—doesn't it feel pretty good to know that you took the high road and did the right thing?

> **Therefore, as God's chosen people, holy and dearly loved, clothe yourselves with compassion, kindness, humility, gentleness and patience. Bear with each other and forgive one another if any of you has a grievance against someone. Forgive as the Lord forgave you. And over all these virtues put on love, which binds them all together in perfect unity.**
> **—Colossians 3:12–14 (NIV)**

Twins of Different Mothers, by Gary

A couple years ago, we suddenly lost a feline member of our family. And, yes, our cats are prominent in our household and very much a part of our family.

Adidas was a shelter rescue that our teenage daughter instantly fell in love with on a trip to PetSmart one day. Despite already having three cats, Tara had poked at the father-daughter soft spot in my heart before I knew it, and I was driving the family back to see her. As Tara already knew, "no" was not a possibility after meeting this kitten looking to escape her lonely cage. After I'd signed a few papers and made a donation, Adidas was on her way to join us in the Cat Palace.

Tara's instincts about Adidas were exceptional, as the cat's cuteness was only exceeded by her sweet personality. Sadly, she developed some medical issues and shockingly passed away way too soon. As those who have suddenly lost a beloved pet know, her sudden passing ripped a void in our household.

While we were still somewhat numb, a sequence of events led us to a small black kitten being showcased for adoption at a local home show. Although my wife was aware of the adoption agency participating in the home show, I had no idea what I was walking into when Beth scored complimentary tickets for the event.

Happily, I can say the rest is history, and that scrawny black kitten became Pippa, the newest occupant of our feline luxury resort. My emotional perspective was to not dishonor Adidas by quickly replacing her, but Beth's persuasiveness and Pippa's persona prevailed.

Reflecting on the circumstances now, it seems to be nothing short of divine intervention. Except for the color difference, Pippa is amazingly similar to Adidas. Her chubby silhouette waddling in the dark with a curled tail tip is the spittin' image of Adidas. She shares the same joy for food and playfulness. There was not and is not a mean bone in either of their bodies. Pippa shares the same love for bird watching and taunting squirrels from our screened-in porch. Both even similarly have enjoyed minicelebrity with their own dedicated Facebook pages.

Importantly, Pippa possesses the same sweet, affectionate disposition. The odds of randomly adopting another cat so strikingly similar are lower than winning the nightly Powerball lottery.

Perhaps very telling and odd at the same time, Pippa immediately meshed with our other four cats. A gradual "everyone get to know each other a little at a time" introductory phase-in period has always been standard—and necessary—protocol. Not this time. Pippa and her four older cat siblings immediately merged into comfortable coexistence as if Pippa were not new at all.

Although Adidas was similarly happy-go-lucky, Pippa seems to take it to the next plateau. She is the feline equivalent of joy personified.

She loves everyone around her. She loves life. Enthusiasm and curiosity abound. Her amber eyes, set against her black velvet fur, peer piercingly from across the room with equal parts wonderment and joy. Somehow you can sense her gaze and suddenly locate her taking a gander your way.

Did I mention that she purrs often? Very often. Perhaps because she possesses a mysterious extrasensory skill reserved for felines, even if Pippa is seemingly snoozing away curled up in a crescent-shaped fur bundle, an audible purr begins as you start making your way toward her from across the room. By the time you reach her, still with eyes shut tight, she has broken into a full-throttle purr. As mentioned, she loves everyone and makes sure to let them know by frequently brushing against them with her internal motor revving in high gear.

Every item in her world is a potential plaything, whether it is a pistachio shell, stray kernel of cat grub, tissue paper, the pen you put down for one second, or some other random object. More traditionally, Pippa also loves her cat toys—until they all need rescuing from under assorted furniture, closed doors, and the fridge.

Just like Adidas, but unlike other cats, she will play fetch and gets kicks from the cat-prank mischief of dropping her toys in the kitty bowls. Pipe cleaners and sponge balls floating in water bowls and commingled in food dishes are a frequent sight in our home. Pippa is even a little tech savvy when it comes to entertainment, enjoying gazing at the action on TV as well as playing the cat version of whack-a-mole on my wife's iPad.

Like all cats, Pippa passionately enjoys her downtime. When she settles in for an obligatory catnap, she's all in, lounging upside down, enjoying the relaxation and rest. Once her internal alarm clock buzzes, she is up in an instant, ready to reengage in the happy pursuit of life. It is off or on, and no in between.

Pippa shares another interesting trait with Adidas. Just like her predecessor, she is frequently on the move, almost seeming a bit omnipresent, popping up wherever you head in the house. Adidas was never found far from the action, and neither is Pippa.

Within the confines of the Cat Palace, Pippa's pursuit of joy finds few limits. As crazy as it sounds, this little cat has provided inspiration for both this book and life in general by exuding joy in all she does. I offer, only half in jest, that Pippa is one of my real-life heroes and role models.

Beyond wanting to model her demeanor and approach to life, those of us around her are blessed. For instance, not surprisingly, it is very difficult not to smile when you are around her...frequently—make that very frequently.

Without question, these feline twins of different mothers have surely brought a lot of joy to our household. And Pippa's just getting started.

Our Nation—The Gift That Keeps On Giving, by Gary

Like our family, a large percentage of those reading this book may fall into the "born and raised here" slice of the American pie. Although we may have been offered glimpses into other world cultures through social-studies classes, TV shows, the evening news, the World Wide Web, periodicals, and international travel, most of us in that slice really, truly only know this nation's one way of life. For those of you who do not fall into that figurative segment and live elsewhere in the world, the opposite may be true.

Surely, the United States of America is large and varied, offering geographic and cultural differences within its expansive boundaries. Additionally, many others from foreign lands have ventured to our nation and have gone through the process to become naturalized citizens, which creates further diversity and broadens our collective culture. Yet, these two phenomena notwithstanding, there is an overarching, pervasive way of life that is uniquely American.

Perhaps most fundamental to defining this broad framework is the notion that we are "the land of the free." We are a country founded on liberties and certain unalienable rights, including the pursuit of happiness. These foundational principles derive from God Himself and His perfect word—the Holy Bible. Our founding fathers were very intentional in creating this blueprint built on bedrock and Christian values, articulated in the Declaration of Independence's most famous phrase:

> "We hold these truths to be self-evident, that all men are created equal, that they are endowed by their Creator with certain unalienable Rights, that among these are Life, Liberty and the pursuit of Happiness."

Seven years later, The Paris Peace Treaty of 1783, which formally ended the Revolutionary War and granted independence to the United States, began with the phrase, "In the name of the most holy and undivided Trinity." This clear Christian reference was further reinforced just before the turn of the nineteenth century when the US Supreme Court officially held the nation to be Christian. Decades later, Congress passed a joint resolution adopting "In God We Trust" as the United States' official motto.

Some might see the notion of America being a Christian nation as a paradox, considering that the First Amendment to our Constitution establishes freedom of religion and speech. Although that core document is silent on God and Christianity, it also fails to mention separation of church and state. Historians indicate that the intent was to clearly allow for the freedom to pursue any religious belief, but retain God as the foundation of the nation. In other words, the founders knew that God's ways—His values and truths—were the perfect principles on which to build a prosperous and just nation.

The foundational principles include the premise that government should be limited, and that it should be of the people and for the people, based on truth and laws. A natural extension of this philosophy is capitalism based on a free-market system. And first and foremost, as previously highlighted, individuals are created equal and have the inalienable rights to life, liberty, and the pursuit of happiness.

These concepts of individual empowerment and limited government gave birth to the American Dream. Broadly, this term has come to signify that individual success, prosperity, and happiness are theoretically attainable by all through individual initiative, hard work, and ambition. Hope prevails.

Many ardently believe that our nation has, in fact, been blessed and has prospered due to these Christian roots as well as our obedience to God's call to be a friend to Israel. Psalm 128:1–2 (ESV) says, "Blessed is everyone who fears the Lord, who walks in his ways! You shall eat the fruit of the labor of your hands; you shall be blessed, and it shall be well with you." Additionally, Jeremiah 29:11 (NIV) reads, "'For I know the plans I have for you,' declares the Lord, 'plans to prosper you and not to harm you, plans to give you hope and a future.'"

In reality, a great many Americans have realized the American Dream to varying degrees. Some have literally gone from rags to riches. Entrepreneurs have flourished through ingenuity and inspiration. Others have climbed ladders of success or realized career achievements through sheer determination and hard work. And yet others have simply experienced happiness and joy through the freedom to pursue their passions and attain personal goals and objectives. Exceptionalism continues to be a hallmark of this nation.

Freedom itself is a tremendous blessing that can easily be taken for granted. It is the norm when you do not know any other way. Having the ability to speak your beliefs without fear or censure, pursue your interests personally and professionally, and choose your friends—and spouse for that matter—all contribute profoundly to happiness.

In America, opportunities and choices abound. Amenities and services are abundant. Although it is right to acknowledge that levels of access and enablers may vary, and like anything involving human beings, faults and flaws exist, our country compares extremely favorably on a global scale. Generosity and human kindness are integral to American society, as is an ongoing aspiration to make our way of life better for all.

Living in this nation, particularly without the contrast of living in another country and culture, can almost make us blind or numb to the awesome privilege it is to be an American. We can easily lose sight of, or perhaps never even set our sights on, how blessed we are to live in this country. In truth, it is a tremendous blessing in and of itself that serves to enable many other blessings.

And these blessings surely help us to realize happiness and joy. It is like the gift that keeps on giving.

Part 3
Finding Joy in Your Life

CHAPTER 13
Deep, Enduring Joy

Reaching Upward for Joy

Perhaps subconsciously symbolically, the heart of this book—the true place these emotions are birthed within us and sent coursing through our bodies—is filled with sources of joy!

We truly hope that these anecdotes and musings seeped into your hearts to stoke your own fond memories and bring to mind personal sources of happiness in your life. It would be our further hope that while you were consuming the content of this book, you began to see the world through a new lens and maybe even to rekindle some of the joys in your life.

Our small family of three has detailed eighty-five sources of joy in our lives. This is surely not an all-encompassing list, as we hardly even broke a sweat coming up with these. We are certain that we could add more with little difficulty—without even counting the many things that continue to elude our heightened consciousness.

Regrettably, our NASCAR pace of life, with its fair share of blown tires, empty fuel tanks, fender benders, and full-scale wrecks, often causes us to overlook the many sources of joy around us. When you're screaming around that ominously banked concrete oval at two hundred miles per hour, jockeying against other doggedly determined drivers, it can be hard to see the butterflies fluttering and hear the birds chirping.

If we recalibrate our thoughts and ways, though, we might tend to slow down time enough to see and experience the things that give us happiness and joy. My epiphany occurred about ten years ago when I truly began to recognize those things, and many more, as blessings.

A critically relevant takeaway is that we are sure you could come up with your own list that might include many of the same items, along with other totally unique ones. Many of them may actively or intermittently be bringing you happiness, if not joy. At the same time, those positive feelings might be covered up by negative emotions occasionally or even frequently. Happiness and joy can easily be smothered by worry, sorrow, anger, bitterness, hurt, loneliness, striving, and more.

The overarching keys to finding more joy can broadly be mapped this way:

1. Recognize the blessings and sources of joy in your life.
2. Live your life in a way that evokes more.
3. Overcome and mitigate the things that steal or smother those good feelings.
4. Find the internal source of joy that prevails through all situations and circumstances.

Sounds simple—or perhaps difficult, depending on your particular station or season in life. Some of this might take a desire to reboot your current mind-set and approach—and then actively work to transform both of them.

Other things are, in fact, simple. They do not require striving. Actually, they are more about resting in what is already done. In some ways you could describe it as "less is more."

There is another profound point to be culled from the NASCAR track metaphor. Oftentimes, we unwittingly place our lives on that oval track to race against the world around us. No matter how fast, how skillfully, or how aggressively we drive, we still end up back in the same place. That somewhat daunting mass of sloped concrete takes us on a perpetual series of left turns to frantically get us back to the same spot—over and over again.

Figuratively, though, when we are grounded by a strong navigation system and purpose, that curved road in front of us straightens. We get off the track and actually go someplace. Our lives find direction, and we head on a journey full of hope and joy.

As mentioned, a pivotal juncture in my life occurred when I truly began recognizing blessings. Really, it was life altering.

The world began looking different. My place in it and my driven nature started to change. The amazing part was that this inherent drive only changed in accordance with the true importance of the task or objective.

The drive remained for things like leading to achieve success at work, deepening my faith, standing up for a cause, and being a good father. Conversely, it largely diminished, or even disappeared, for things that were pretty much meaningless in the grand scheme. The competitive drive that accompanied me in sports to the point of unhealthiness largely left me.

Clearly my priorities changed, but it was more than that. Perhaps it was that I no longer attached my own stature or even self-worth to the outcome of a sporting event, having the highest batting average, or winning a trophy. I never consciously looked at sports that way, but it seems apparent now that some of that mentality must have been mixed up in my competitive spirit. Outwardly I didn't desire to bask in the limelight, but inwardly I had a need for others to recognize my value. It made me feel safe to have objective evidence and not be vulnerable to subjective opinions or whims.

Notably, I came to realize that I wasn't really accomplishing those things on my own anyway. And when I turned my attention to the One who really was enabling them, it was very freeing.

Journeying through life recognizing the blessings rather than grumbling about the little inconveniences or even the sharp, sweeping curveballs thrown your way changes your entire outlook and mood.

Like every other one, our family has worked through many challenges and heartaches, but this in no way diminishes our sense of the rich blessings. Failing to recognize them inhibits our ability to live life to the fullest, while counting them allows us to extract happiness and joy each day in the journey.

For a number of years, Beth and Tara would go through an exercise before bed of naming their highs and lows for the day. The lows called out the things that might require support and ministering, while the highs drew attention to the blessings. What a simple exercise, but also a very powerful one at the same time to shift our outlook.

And, perhaps most importantly, recognizing the true source of good things and happenings actually broadens your perspective. It literally takes you higher in your vantage point, moving from an earthly, human view to a heavenly view.

Positioning for Happiness

The people around us can have a profound impact on our own level of happiness. Let's face it, hanging around with others who possess a sour disposition, bitterness, questionable values, or a negative outlook typically brings you down with them.

We have all encountered the person who delights in cracking insults disguised as jokes and who is capable of turning any discussion into a complaint session or sea of antipathy. As though this attitude were a virulent disease, others quickly find themselves falling prey to it.

Conversely, surrounding ourselves with upbeat, caring people supports and elevates our own outlook. Spending time with high-integrity, joyful people powerfully plays into our own demeanor. When everyone else around you sees the glass half-full, it tends to transform any inclination for a half-empty view. Consciously or subconsciously, we watch those individuals, usually with admiration, and begin to model the same behavior.

A key to living with greater happiness and joy lies in placing ourselves among the right individuals. Oftentimes we can make conscious choices about with whom we associate. Intentionally surrounding ourselves with positive influences, particularly those who radiate joy, almost surely will lift our own level of happiness.

Sometimes, though, it can be very difficult to distance ourselves or even disassociate from the less-than-positive people because they might be family members, teammates, coworkers, or part of some other group affiliation. In these cases, the choice might be to find ways to actively guard your own mind-set, limit your interactions as best you can, address things directly, or influence change through your own example. (In an extreme case, living with others who are hostile or abusive surely warrants actively working at transformation or removing yourself from the relationship.)

Additionally, the character of the people within your life circles can dramatically define the support systems around you. In times of need and trouble, those skewed to the more positive, cheerful end of the personality spectrum are more apt to offer a helping hand, an encouraging word, or a sympathetic ear.

Surely, this is not to suggest that you attempt to surround yourself only with perfect people—they do not exist. Everyone has their shortcomings and errs in their ways, but with a little grace all the way around, we can surely see a contrast between the various personalities in our lives.

All in all, if we look at our waking hours as a pie chart, the bigger the portion spent with those positive influencers and role models, the better we are positioned for happiness. If the time spent with the alternative cast of characters is a mere slice, you likely flash smiles pretty regularly through the course of each day.

Simply put, the company we keep contributes to our level of happiness and the frequency with which we experience it.

Mentality Matters

Surely, there is truth in the notion that the way we choose our company impacts our own thought process and approach to life. But, ultimately, it begins and ends within our own hearts and minds.

As stated in the opening of the book, when it comes to finding happiness and joy in our lives, there is no getting around it—our mentality matters!

We can significantly shape our experience in life according to the way we approach it. Do we start with a mind-set of thanksgiving and appreciation for the blessings in our lives? Is our starting point cheerful or dour? Do we look for the good and work to overcome the not so good?

When we approach life with both a positive attitude and positive expectations, happiness and success more readily follow. This is not wishful thinking or some new-age practice, but rather a correlation that has been proven through many studies as well as collective experiences.

Pursuing life with a finger on the trigger of judgment has a way of causing us to shoot ourselves in the foot. When we look for the bad, we can usually find it—even if it requires some convoluted reasoning. Some view finding the dark cloud around every silver lining as virtuous realism and perspective. There is a place for balance, but this mind-set is like a bucket of cold water waiting to douse the flames of happiness.

Instead, we can choose to look for the good in every person and situation. And guess what? It is almost always there to be spotted. This practice does not make you delusional; it only shifts your vantage point. The more we get in the habit of shifting our vantage point, the more natural it becomes—and the more our mood lifts.

The impact does not all happen within our heads and hearts, though. As we naturally see the good around us, we become ambassadors of goodwill. We become conciliators. We offer words of encouragement that lift spirits, instill happiness, and evoke joy. The atmosphere shifts, returning to us in the form of our own greater happiness.

The other half of the positive-thinking equation to pair with a positive attitude is positive expectation. Just like when we look for the good, when we expect good outcomes, they are much more likely to happen. Of course, beauty is in the eye of the beholder, so this is also impacted by our perspective in evaluating the outcome.

This is not to suggest that we can blindly journey through life, cutting corners and making poor choices, hoping that everything will magically work out. Sometimes things will work out, but more often it requires us to do our part. Maintaining optimism actually directly and indirectly influences the process, our performance, the support we receive, and others' perceptions. Accordingly, the probability of success or achieving the desired outcome rises substantially.

Many athletes provide testimony to this phenomenon. Russia pioneered the practice of visualization in 1984 to improve the performance of its athletic teams. Since then, many elite athletes including Jack Nicklaus, Michael Jordan, and Tiger Woods have credited this practice for the success they have achieved in their careers.

Visualization can be briefly described as forming images in your mind of performing the right technique and achieving success. Specifically, for those athletes it would include sinking a birdie putt to win a tournament or nailing a three-pointer at the buzzer to win the championship.

By simply envisioning success and bathing their minds with this imagery beforehand, those athletes were able to realize their lofty aspirations. Surely, their accomplishments also required a great deal of talent, but the key point is that they better positioned themselves for success—as well as happiness and joy!

As Norman Vincent Peale wrote and preached about the power of positive thinking, he encountered critics and naysayers who attempted to discredit his work. Those arguments were often obtuse and weak, but he heeded his own advice and stayed the course to transform countless lives. More than seven million copies of *The Power of Positive Thinking* have been sold, and some multiple of that number have read the book or heard Peale's teachings, but the endless testimonials offer the best evidence that a positive outlook improves our lives.

The Reverend Billy Graham, who has been referred to as "America's pastor" due to his enormous following and stellar reputation, has long been an ardent supporter of Peale. More than five decades ago, Reverend Graham identified Dr. Peale and his wife, Ruth, as having done more for the Kingdom of God than anyone he knew and lauded the tremendous encouragement they provided to him personally.

That is some pretty lofty praise from one of the most wise and respected leaders in our country's history. I think he would agree—mentality matters!

CHAPTER 14
Christianity, Creation, and the Cosmos

Searching for Purpose and Meaning

Although it was not reflected earlier in this book because my personal backstory picked up later in life, I grew up in a Christian household. Attendance and involvement in church were not an option, but rather a mandate. Our family members were faithful participants in all that the church had to offer—Sunday school, vacation Bible school, church consistory, events, fundraisers, choir, junior choir, youth fellowship, the softball team, Bible studies, and of course, church services themselves.

Perhaps pondering the awe-inspiring omnipotence of God and all creation—or the fact that I was simply wired to be a deep thinker (or both)—led me to contemplate the incomprehensibility of it all. From as far back as I can recall, I actively sought to make the infinite finite and the incomprehensible comprehensible.

Despite the vast complexity of it all, my logical brain wanted to solve the mystery—and perhaps take the jump out of the "leap of faith." Much to my parents' chagrin, not to mention the almost impossible challenge to appease me with a sufficiently satisfying answer, spiritual questions such as the following abounded:

1. If God created the universe, who created God?
2. How could God be three people all in one—the Father, Jesus, and the Holy Spirit?
3. Is God mean or loving?
4. Why are we here? What is the meaning and purpose of it all?
5. How much more good than bad will it take to get into Heaven?

And on a scientific level, many other questions persisted:

1. How would it even be conceivable that a big bang in nothingness evolved into the incredibly vast and intricate universe?
2. How is it possible for the millions and millions of variables to align to create and sustain life?
3. How did the gases even exist to create a big bang?
4. What makes people tick?
5. What motivates each of us to take different paths, have different preferences, and make widely varying choices?
6. Why are some able to live with happiness and joy?

This ongoing search to make sense out of the intangible and abstract likely had something to do with me initially electing psychology as my college major. This eventually changed, either because I preferred to forego the gruesome cruelty of injecting laboratory rats to pass the required clinical psychology courses, because I didn't envision spending my career trying to answer the same questions for others that I was still seeking on my own, or simply because I turned my study of human behavior toward marketing—the more enterprising, capitalistic underpinning of every business.

While I came to accept that God's plan and omnipotence were not meant to be understood, it was easy to rule out the explanations offered by the science community due to the sheer mathematical improbability of the underlying hypotheses. The former is a grand plan by an omnipotent Creator, and the latter is a confluence of randomness. It simply became my choice to abandon these questions in favor of the proverbial leap of faith.

Make no mistake about it, though, I have always believed in God and that He supernaturally sent His only begotten Son to live as man among us. It was just that I hoped to build a mental bridge that made it much easier to get from point A to point B.

The Good News

It wasn't until many years later that I began to really fully connect the dots. Differences in people, situations, and lives were not all chalked up to human psychology, chance, or circumstance.

Most importantly, I came to realize that God was not this distant Creator, watching us play out our lives on earth from on high. Instead, He is our loving Heavenly Father who longingly wants to know and be known by us.

In His marvelously brilliant and perfect plan, which was incredibly foreshadowed throughout the Bible's Old Testament, our Heavenly Father sent Jesus to be the way, the truth, and the life in a broken world. By manifest destiny, Jesus died a brutal death, rose from the dead, and ascended to heaven to erase all our sins and reconcile us with our perfect Maker.

This profound event literally changed everything forevermore. It is the single greatest act of love in the course of human history.

For believers, the key to eternal life went from "do" to "done."

No longer would we be captives to endless striving to *do* enough good to earn a place in heaven. Such a scenario is wrought with uncertainty and angst, particularly considering our imperfect human nature and habitual sin. The line of demarcation was unknown and the alternative a fiery pit of suffering.

Instead, we are offered grace through faith. All our past, present, and future sins are forgiven through what was *done* by Jesus as humankind's sacrificial lamb. We suddenly are transformed from flawed to flawless.

This grace in forgiving our sins offers eternal life in heaven through one specific act of *faith*—acknowledging Jesus as our Lord and Savior and repenting for our sins. As true believers, we instantly become children of God and know with absolute assurance that when our time is up in this world, we will live eternally in the Heavenly Kingdom.

As unbelievably awesome as this is, it gets even better!

God loves each one of us more than we can even comprehend and wants to be an active part of our lives. He wants to prosper and bless us. He wants to commune with us and build an intimate one-on-one relationship with all of His children.

God doesn't just want to get us to heaven—He also wants to get heaven into us!

When Jesus rose from the dead to take His place with our Heavenly Father, He sent His very own spirit, which healed the sick and raised the dead to live within all believers. The Holy Spirit dwells within us to connect us to the Father and Son and renew our hearts.

Fruit of the Spirit

The Holy Spirit living within us serves as an advocate, helper, and compass to live in righteousness. This indwelling works to transform us from the inside out, developing nine attributes that the Bible refers to as the fruit of the spirit: love, joy, peace, patience, kindness, goodness, faithfulness, gentleness, and self-control.

It does not require a brilliant psychologist or mathematician to draw a correlation between all these attributes and happiness. As can be seen in the preceding pages of this book, all of them contribute to personal happiness directly and indirectly in many ways.

Of course, joy is joy.

No Greater Joy

As previously detailed within the pages of this book, each of us can proactively work to bring happiness and joy into our lives. The pursuit of happiness becomes attainable through our choices, mind-set, and the people we place around us. The elusive carrot that otherwise dangles tantalizingly beyond our reach suddenly moves within arm's reach.

We have dedicated a couple hundred pages to encourage everyone to recognize these truths and to choose the pathways to joy. Blessings can be found all around us, and once we routinely recognize and embrace them, happiness and joy tend to follow.

Although our approaches, attitudes, and choices can surely contribute to experiencing happiness and joy, the ultimate joy is found in the Lord. It is a joy that sustains itself through time and all circumstances.

Most fundamentally, simply having the truth planted in your heart that God is real, sees the good in us, loves us deeply, and has made an eternal place for us in heaven surely is reason to live every day, every moment, with joy. Knowing that He is indeed an awesome, omnipresent Father interested in even the smallest details of our lives provides reason to rejoice from the rooftops.

Kay Warren, cofounder of Saddleback Church in Lake Forest, California along with her husband and renowned author, Rick Warren, defines joy like this: "Joy is the settled assurance that God is in control of all the details of my life, the quiet confidence that ultimately everything is going to be alright, and the determined choice to praise God in every situation."

One the most powerfully promising and instructive sentences in the entire Bible is Proverbs 3:5–6 (NIV), which reads, "Trust in the Lord with all your heart and lean not on your own understanding; in all your ways submit to him, and he will make your paths straight."

We do have free will in our lives, but knowing that our Heavenly Father has us figuratively in His hands frees us from anxiety and worry. Although we have encountered, and will continue to encounter, troubles in this world, we can rest in Him and the promise of eternal life.

As we place our unwavering trust in the Lord, the weight of troubles and burdens is cast off our shoulders, allowing us to focus on living life to its fullest. We can turn our attention toward finding the joy all around us, which interestingly also comes with bringing joy to others.

This undeniable inner joy sustains itself, allowing us to fully experience external sources of joy and bridge us over its temporal nature. The exhilarating peaks remain, but the free falls into the depths of the valleys disappear.

Beth wrote the following essay describing how her life has been transformed through the joy of the Lord.

Joy from the Lord, by Beth

To the best of my ability, I try to begin each day on a positive note. Most days I find myself thanking God as I am getting out of bed. In my mind I review the words to Psalm 118:24 (ESV), "This is the day the Lord has made, let us rejoice and be glad in it." Sometimes the melody from the children's song of this verse goes through my mind and I mentally sing this scripture as I head to the shower.

As a disclaimer, I was not born with an innate positive bent or personality. On the contrary, if I am not mindful, I tend to see the negative side of things before the positive. I believe this character trait has been with me since childhood. Evidence of this is seen in numerous photos of me as a child. My lack of a smile is an obvious feature in many of these captured memories. Despite the story portrayed in my family photo albums, I was raised in a loving home and have many positive memories of my childhood. These opposing facts support my belief that leaning toward the somber end of the spectrum is natural for me.

I detailed the above personal reflection only because my natural bent does not lend itself to waking up with joy in my heart. As a young adult, I quickly realized it would be beneficial for me to try to overcome this tendency. To do this I turned to a genre of books often referred to at the time as self-help books. Advice from both Wayne Dyer and Dale Carnegie was contemplated as I tried to fix what I saw as broken in myself.

One life principle that has stayed with me from that time is from Dale Carnegie. He taught the benefit of facing one day at a time, not looking forward with worry or backward with regret. He used an illustration about a ship to explain this teaching. As a ship has compartments that can be sealed to prevent water in one compartment from flooding another, so too do we need to seal off the past and the future. He wrote, "We cannot live one moment in either of those eternities and to try to so do could ruin both our minds and bodies. We can be content to live the only time we possibly can—today."

The Bible teaches a similar lesson in Matthew 6:34 (NIV): "Therefore do not worry about tomorrow, for tomorrow will worry about itself. Each day has enough trouble of its own." Thankfully this teaching and all the wisdom from this living book became my ultimate self-help guide when I was in my twenties. As I allowed the Word to shape my thoughts and beliefs, I started changing from the inside out. I didn't need formulas or a three-step plan to fix me, only time spent with God and His Word.

The reason I am now able to wake up with joy in my heart is not because of pop psychology, but instead because I found the true source of joy. Joy is one of the many gifts we receive from God as we grow in our comprehension of His love, His goodness, and His grace.

Avoiding the Thieves of Joy

Although it would be wrong to suggest that troubles will simply disappear when we find the Lord, it is fair to say that our ability to persevere through hardships and rebound from difficulties improves significantly. We live in a broken world, and the very nature of this life entails problems, heartaches, and sorrow.

But as regrettably real as this may be, the presence of God in our lives changes the way we experience difficulties, our ability to recover, and our ongoing outlook. We gain perspective and hope by simply knowing who He is and His promise to us.

Beyond the inherent peace and joy brought by the Holy Spirit, we are greatly comforted by knowing how much our Heavenly Father loves us and has plans to prosper and bless us. Jeremiah 29:11 (NIV) says, "'For I know the plans I have for you,' declares the Lord, 'plans to prosper you and not to harm you, plans to give you hope and a future.'"

We also know that He will never forsake us. We can count on His goodness and faithfulness even in times of trouble. God is love. Psalm 30:5 (NKJV) says, "Weeping may endure for a night, but joy comes in the morning." In other words, even though times are tough at the moment, there is reason to rejoice because He will soon help us find joy.

Sometimes our joy is robbed by events or occurrences that have not even happened, but rather that we fear or worry might happen. Anxiety can oftentimes be the largest wet blanket over our flames of happiness. Negative scenarios can be endless in our minds and hover over us like a dark cloud of despair.

Discernment guides us to avoid difficulties by making good choices and prompting us to be proactive in our lives. Conversely, worry essentially turns even the most remote possibilities into emotional reality by pulling them forward into our minds. Jesus boldly instructed us, "Therefore do not worry about tomorrow, for tomorrow will worry about itself. Each day has enough trouble of its own" (Matthew 6:34 NIV).

Living our lives this way allows us to peel back the wet blanket of worry, opening us to see the blessings around us and feel happiness. Jesus also provided this direction about worry, knowing that we have the same awesome, loving Father ultimately looking out for us.

Other barriers to happiness and joy are sin and shame. Sometimes our own voice of self-condemnation can be the loudest and most controlling of all. Jesus healed the sick and raised the dead, so He surely had the power to avoid His humanly fate, but instead He chose to take all our sins and shame to the cross—past, present, and future.

The moment we become sons and daughters of the Kingdom, the slate is wiped clean, and our hearts are renewed. We are given a fresh start and no longer need to be prisoners of the past. With any lingering guilt lifted off our shoulders, we are set free to pursue and experience joy.

Sometimes, it is the flip scenario that robs our joy. Holding on to bitterness and refusing to forgive others hurts us more than it does the perceived offenders. These negative emotions often stand in the way of our own happiness. Just like He forgave us completely, God calls us to do the same with others.

It not only makes logical and moral sense to demonstrate the same grace that has been extended to us, but it also provides a positive impact on our own mind-set. Carrying around resentment and anger only serves to hold on to the pain of the past. In accounting terms, eliminating these emotional debits allows our account balance of happiness to rise.

Even the specter of death itself is experienced very differently. We inherently want to remain in this world along with our loved ones, but the inevitability of death no longer is something to be feared when we know eternal life in heaven awaits us. 1 Corinthians 15:55 (NLT) states it this way: "O death, where is your victory? O death, where is your sting?"

> Philippians 4:4–7 (NIV) says,
> *Rejoice in the Lord always. I will say it again: Rejoice! Let your gentleness be evident to all. The Lord is near. Do not be anxious about anything, but in every situation, by prayer and petition, with thanksgiving, present your requests to God. And the peace of God, which transcends all understanding, will guard your hearts and your minds in Christ Jesus.*

And Psalm 46:1 (NLT) says, "God is our refuge and strength, always ready to help in times of trouble."

Overcoming Sorrow

One of the most pervasive thieves of joy is the sorrow associated with losing a loved one. The pain and loneliness can be all consuming, suffocating any feelings of happiness and joy.

Unfortunately, death is a part of life—at least in this world.

As much as it is the reality for every one of us on planet earth, losing those around us who share our lives and whom we love is very difficult. For this reason, Jesus gave us specific direction to care for the widows and orphans, as they are particularly vulnerable.

Understanding that we are just passing through a temporal world helps, especially when you have given yourself to our Lord and Savior. Knowing you are a mere visitor here and a citizen of the Heavenly Kingdom provides perspective. It promises there is more to come after your time in this world ends.

The practical reality, though, is that a void is created when someone close to us passes on. When someone whom you loved, who shared life with you and maybe offered a sense of security, or who perhaps even provided for you is suddenly gone, it is natural to feel loneliness and sorrow. It requires recalibrating and finding a new normal.

When we center our lives on God, we realize that we are secure in Him for eternity. We know that we are never alone and He is always there for us. Instead of loneliness, we feel His love and an almost unexplainable internal peace.

The ultimate scenario is living each day fearlessly to its fullest and extracting joy in this world, comforted by knowing that when our time has come we will be reunited with our loved ones in a joyous heavenly home.

Over the past few years, Beth and I have lost three of our parents. Each of them lived a good, full life, but it still hurts for them to be gone. Although these losses remain relatively recent, we live joyously—not because we did not love our parents deeply, but because our foundation is built on the Lord.

In awesome acts of love and kindness, God showed us in three separate dreams and through prayer that each one of them is living joyously with Him in heaven! What an incredible blessing and amazing testimony to our Heavenly Father's goodness! We surely miss them, but we are thrilled to know we will be with them again on the other side of eternity.

Not everyone may be comforted in this same way, but it should be comforting to know that this is the heart of the Father. This is His grand design, and it offers everlasting life with Him in a world filled with joy!

Joy in the Morning, by Gary

Well chronicled within this book is our love for our cats and their prominence in our household. Sadly, we unexpectedly lost one of our five feline family members as we were finalizing this book and beginning the publishing process.

Fila, our ruggedly handsome boy, suddenly stopped eating and became lethargic. A trip to the vet revealed that he was experiencing kidney failure. His condition quickly worsened, and he was admitted to an animal hospital specializing in internal medicine. A week later, the doctors were out of treatment options, so we resigned ourselves to bringing him home to provide direct loving care and pray for a miracle.

For three days, I remained by his side, attempting to comfort him. Every hour that passed, the prospects of a miracle seemed to diminish as we sadly watched his body shut down. In one regard, it was heartbreaking to hold him as he expelled his last breath. This was softened, though, by the undeniable expressions of love that were exchanged through this difficult time. Of course, my full desire was for a miracle recovery, but almost paradoxically, those last few days were simultaneously heartbreaking and special.

Like the midday news program featuring a panel of four women and one man, Fila was also OUTNUMBERED in our household. He was the sole male among a gaggle of five felines residing in the Cat Palace. This did not deter him from being front and center for every formal and informal event or gathering in our home. If something was going on, Fila could be located with a quick turn of the head or by recasting of your sight line.

Fila was a creature of habit, but never refrained from being a trendsetter or a copycat. He took special delight in finding and quickly occupying new spots to hang out, whether it were the just-opened FedEx delivery box, a new blanket, a piece of clothing dropped on the floor, an open suitcase, a new piece of furniture, or a soon-to-be-filled serving bowl. (As a quick reassurance to previous and future guests and to alleviate any fears of cat hair or kitty litter consumption, all such bowls receive a thorough washing prior to being filled with food.)

He gladly accepted the role as unofficial "spokescat" to remind us that mealtime was fast approaching. The process always began with an unwavering stare that progressively moved to closer proximity to ensure he had our attention, and then was typically capped off with some gentle utterances when we failed to act on his suggestion.

Perhaps Fila's favorite habit or tradition was to tightly tuck himself under my arm for an evening catnap or some serious REM sleep through the night. Much like his mealtime duties, and almost always like clockwork, he would summon me from my end-of-evening slumber on the couch so he could settle in for some restorative sleep.

The combination of his sudden loss and the manner in which it played out had me feeling particularly sorrowful. At the same time as his passing, we learned that another one of our cats was experiencing her own early-stage kidney failure like two of our other cats. A couple days later, with the events of the previous ten days in my mind, I felt a sudden compulsion to embark on a mission to find some new special-formula food that would not cause our cats to turn their noses in the air.

After having little luck, I planned to head home and order the food online. As I was driving out of the shopping center, I called a last-second audible and veered straight to take one last shot at another pet store across the street. With head down and determination to limit additional unfruitful time, I quickly made my way to the cat-food section in the back of the store. After a brief look and some assistance from a sales associate, it was apparent that my Saturday morning mission would be unsuccessful.

A funny thing happened, though, as I briskly walked back to the front of the store to head home. An image caught my attention out of the corner of my left eye. Lounging on top of one of those burlap-wrapped and carpeted cat towers appeared to be a miniature replica of Fila. A local feline adoption agency had set up shop for the morning in hopes of finding homes for a small number of kittens.

A couple photos and a return visit later, Beth and I found ourselves filling out paperwork to take Bella home. She was bursting with personality and took a quick liking to us. Although we clearly had no thoughts of seeking another cat when the day began, considering that the only kitten that fell within my sights on the impromptu trip bore a quite remarkable resemblance to a young Fila, it seemed clear to us that she was destined for the Cat Palace.

Incredibly similarly to when we found Pippa after the loss of our cat Adidas, Bella quickly integrated into our household and has been a true joy! And, much like Pippa, her overall demeanor and upbeat presence exude joy.

Although we still miss Fila and possess many fond memories of him, Bella has been another perfectly timed gift to heal our hearts and backfill the space with joy. Much like the promise of God stated in Psalm 30:5 (NLT), "Weeping may last through the night, but joy comes with the morning," the darkness of Fila's death was lightened with the morning sun of Bella.

Change, the Enemy of Joy

A natural enemy of joy can be change. When we hit high points in our lives, we would like to linger in those places.

The world keeps turning and time marches on, though, and sometimes, unfortunately, good circumstances change for and around us. Of course, the opposite can be said, whereby circumstances change for the better when we hit low points or are aspiring for more.

However, the point here is that we can't really bottle up happiness or joy from different events or times in our lives to drink in later. We do to a small degree by retaining videos, photographs, journals, and other mementos that allow us to revisit those good memories from the past. These items can serve as reminders, almost like bookmarks of our lives, bringing back great memories and even calling up the emotions we felt at the time.

Regrettably, the phenomenon is temporal and can wear off quickly. And the more frequently we revisit the past, the less intense the feelings. The law of diminishing returns throws cold water on the smoldering coals.

A wise philosopher once said, "The only constant in life is change." This is not totally true for everyone, but it is fundamentally right on point.

Beyond the impact of moving us out of the happy times and places in our lives, change presents an ever-evolving array of new challenges to tackle and circumstances for which to adapt. This can rob us of happiness and joy as we become preoccupied with, or even anxious about, navigating the new terrain.

Our relationship with God equips us to better deal with change. Rather than being mired in worry or anxiety, we can step into change with the confidence of knowing that God is both with us and ahead of us in our journey.

Also, importantly, Romans 8:28 (NLT) tells us, "And we know that God causes everything to work together for the good of those who love God and are called according to his purpose for them." This assurance might even have the impact of transposing angst and adventure.

Most everything in life is subject to changing, but not everything. God is the same yesterday, today, and tomorrow.

And because we can't really bottle up the high points to relive repeatedly, augmenting those moments with a sustainable source of joy neutralizes the thief of change.

A few years ago, during a season of difficult change that included the death of Beth's mother and a relocation from our Charlotte home, which we loved, to a cold, blustery, snow-laden northern city, God showed her a means to cope, adapt, and heal. The following essay details His "Five R" formula for that period and beyond.

> **Jesus Christ is the same yesterday and today and forever.**
> —Hebrews 13:8 (NIV)

> **"I am the Alpha and the Omega—the beginning and the end," says the Lord God. "I am the one who is, who always was, and who is still to come—the Almighty One."**
> —Revelation 1:8 (NLT)

God's Five Rs of Relief, by Beth

As I write this and reflect on our journey these past few months, I am reminded how God is always doing something new in our lives. Our lives are filled with definite seasons. We not only have the seasons represented on our calendars, but we have personal seasons where our responsibilities and roles change. Some of these personal seasons last for years, such as the season of raising our children. Some seasons are very short, lasting only weeks or months, as when we find ourselves having to relocate for a job or recuperate from an injury.

I believe God gave us both types of seasons as a source of joy and blessings. He knows change is good and inspiring for us. Seasons marking our calendar often bless us with different temperatures and weather patterns, as well as changes in the number of daylight hours. If we live in an area with marked seasonal changes, we can cozy up to the fireplace in the dark, cold, longer nights of winter as well as bask in the sunshine on the hot, lazy days of summer. Having both allows us to appreciate each all the more.

Some seasons can be especially stressful when we are asked to take on more than seems humanly possible to handle. If you find yourself in a particularly busy season of life, I believe God will give you the grace to handle your responsibilities until the season is over. A few years ago, God blessed me by showing me four things we can do when we face the busy seasons in our lives. By making these practices a part of our daily lives, we will reduce our stress levels as well as stay connected to God.

Remember + Recharge + Refocus + Rely = Relief

Remember: We must purposely remember the God whom we serve. "Be strong and courageous. Do not be afraid; do not be discouraged, for the Lord your God will be with you wherever you go" (Joshua 1:9 NIV). No matter how stressful our days become, we are never alone. God is walking with us, guiding us, and providing us with the strength we need to see us through whatever we are facing. Also, reflecting on ways God has seen us through other stress-filled times in our lives will help give us the perspective that this too shall pass.

Recharge: We need to allow ourselves time to relax and take breaks from our daily responsibilities. This means time for fun things that bring us joy as well as time with God, to allow Him to refresh us. "But Jesus often withdrew to lonely places and prayed" (Luke 5:16 NIV). If taking time to pray was important for Jesus to fit into His busy days, imagine how much more so it is for us! Our time with God should be guarded and prioritized. The little things that bring joy to our lives, such as spending time with family and friends or enjoying our favorite hobby, are also very important. Even if our busy days allow us only brief moments of our favorite activities, these small bits of refreshing will ease our stress levels. Thankfully, as with nature, seasons change, and as our schedules ease up, we will most likely be able to enjoy more of our favorite pastimes.

Refocus: We need to find someone else to think about besides ourselves, someone whom we can bless. "For we are God's handiwork, created in Christ Jesus to do good works, which God prepared in advance for us to do" (Ephesians 2:10 NIV). This verse clearly calls us to serve others, so we must guard against letting our busy lives prevent us from doing this work. It may be providing a listening ear for a hurting friend. Or perhaps it can be as simple as an encouraging word to someone on Facebook. This may be the hardest of the practices to implement. We often find it hard to justify taking the time to add something else to our to-do list when our schedules are already overcrowded. However, as God has called us to do this, He will also provide us the ability to carry it out.

Rely: We must choose to rely on God as we face the uncertainties in our lives. Stressful times can often cause us to think the worst about situations and easily feel overwhelmed by our day-to-day struggles. We must rely on God's goodness; everything that has come into our lives has passed through the filter of His loving hands. "And we know that in all things God works for the good of those who love him, who have been called according to his purpose" (Romans 8:28 NIV). We must also rely on His strength; no problem we face is too big for God. "So do not fear, for I am with you; do not be dismayed, for I am your God. I will strengthen you and help you; I will uphold you with my righteous right hand" (Isaiah 41:10 NIV). Lastly, we must rely on His love for us. "For I am convinced that neither death nor life, neither angels nor demons, neither the present nor the future, nor any powers, neither height nor depth, nor anything else in all creation, will be able to separate us from the love of God that is in Christ Jesus our Lord" (Romans 8:38–39 NIV).

As inhabitants of this world, we are going to have problems and struggles, as well as seasons with more challenges and difficulties. In fact, Jesus himself told us that in this world, we will have trouble. Thankfully we have someone we can turn to for help. When you feel stressed, overwhelmed, and beaten up by this world, turn to Him. He is always listening, and He has all the answers. "Come to me all you who are weary and burdened, and I will give you rest" (Matthew 11:28 NIV).

> **The precepts of the Lord are right, giving joy to the heart. The commands of the Lord are radiant, giving light to the eyes.**
> **—Psalm 19:8 (NIV)**

CHAPTER 15
Deepening Your Relationship with God

A Deepened Relationship through the Word

Deepening our rapport with God works to elevate our happiness and joy even higher. A strong, impenetrable relationship serves to guard us further against detractors. It also enables a greater manifestation of the fruit of the Spirit, including pervasive feelings of peace and joy.

One of my favorite biblical metaphors is that of a tree planted by streams of water. A firmly rooted tree stands tall, is adorned with abundant leaves, and always produces fruit. In nature, for instance, the deeper and wider the roots of an oak tree, the more majestic and enduring the tree is.

God works the same way. The unseen roots represent our grounding in the Word and our relationship with the Lord, nourished by the living waters of the Holy Spirit. The more grounded we are with deep roots, the more we are fed by the living waters, and the greater our vitality, splendor, and strength. Deep roots allow us not only to prevail through the storms of this world, but also to bear fruit through all circumstances.

> Jeremiah 17:7–8 (NIV) reads,
> *But blessed is the one who trusts in the Lord, whose confidence is in him. They will be like a tree planted by the water that sends out its roots by the stream. It does not fear when heat comes; its leaves are always green. It has no worries in a year of drought and never fails to bear fruit.*

> Psalm 1:1–3 (NIV) declares,
> *Blessed is the one who does not walk in step with the wicked or stand in the way that sinners take or sit in the company of mockers, but whose delight is in the law of the Lord, and who meditates on his law day and night. That person is like a tree planted by streams of water, which yields its fruit in season and whose leaf does not wither—whatever they do prospers.*

As in any relationship, the more time you spend together and get to know each other, the closer you become. One great way to get to know God better is to read the Bible—or "the Word" or "the Truth" as it is often referred to within its pages.

Through reading and studying these pages, we learn who God is, what He has done, what He promises, what He calls us to do, and so much more. The Word reveals the Father's heart, Jesus as the perfect role model, and the Holy Spirit's ongoing, omnipresent influence on humanity. It provides answers and insights to the mysteries around us. This perfect book, completely inspired by God Himself, encourages us and gives us hope.

The more we read the Bible, the more the truth is captured within us. The Holy Spirit helps us understand, absorb, and retain these scriptures, etching them on our hearts. Simultaneously, these "God-breathed" words help to renew our minds to align with our hearts.

As part of this collaborative initiative, Beth identified reading books and stories as a great source of joy in her life. (Our overflowing bookcases bear testimony to this truth.) We have chosen to include this essay in the conclusion because it directly speaks to the most magnificent book of all time, which weaves together many stories to form the ultimate love story. And like our book, it was a collaborative effort with divine direction.

The Joy of a Story, by Beth

Stories—they are loved by most everyone in their varying forms and are an integral part of our lives. Our first experience with a story may happen as early as the day we are born. Our first story might sound something like this: "Hi, beautiful. I am your mommy, and this is your daddy. We are going to have a wonderful life together. We love you so very much." All too quickly this same baby will be begging for one more story as a wearied parent rereads a favorite book again and again. As we journey through life, new stories are discovered by us every day, and without realizing it, we are creating our very own story, written day by day, as we spend time on planet earth.

I am an avid reader and collector of books. When I was a young girl, library day was a high point in my week. I was always excited to find new books, and I never left without the maximum number of allowed books secured away in my book bag. As an adult I have a somewhat extensive collection of books in a variety of different genres. I enjoy both fiction and nonfiction, trivial subjects and those that are thought provoking. I can find joy in books written to inspire laughter, as well as those designed to bring one to tears. Thanks to Tara coming into our lives, our home also contains a collection of children's books. Here among the color-filled illustrations, the joy of a story can be found quite easily by all ages, as long as one is open to this possibility.

We get drawn into stories as we watch our TVs or peruse our computer's news feed. We share and listen to them as we gather for lunch with coworkers or friends. We read the story of others' lives, often in real time, as we scroll through our social media feeds. We bless our family members by sharing our intimate stories as we gather around our kitchen tables or relax in our family rooms.

God understands our love of stories. How could He not? He created us. He also created the most intricate and beautiful love story ever written, His Word, the Bible. Starting in Genesis with the story of creation, through His ultimate act of love for us on the cross, recounted in the Gospels, and ending with the future completion of His story foretold in Revelation, His love shines through and permeates every page. In its entirety it is a love story that, when unfolded, gives us the greatest story of all time—God's plan for restoring a family to Himself. Within the grand story of His love for us, we find recounted the life stories of pillars of faith, as well as those of average faith or no faith. We also find beautiful parables, stories authored by God. All of these interwoven stories are designed to teach us, inspire us, warn us, encourage us, and give us joy. He truly is the master storyteller and the author of joy. Here within the pages of His book, we will grow to know Him.

The book you are holding in your hands is a collection of stories—stories about our family and the blessings we find around us that bring us joy. I hope you have found joy in reading our stories. More so, I hope from reading them, you find yourself experiencing a bit more joy in the daily story of your life.

A Deepened Relationship through Friendship and Intimacy

We further build our relationship with God by spending additional time together. This can be a formal, dedicated time of prayer as well as informal conversations throughout the normal course of your day.

If this verbiage seems a little strange to some of you, it may be that you have been missing an extraordinary opportunity. God loves to hear our praise and appreciation just like any parent would want to hear from his or her children. He is also there to receive our petitions. And, importantly, He also speaks directly to us if we open ourselves to hear.

Psalm 46:10 (NIV) says, "Be still, and know that I am God." If it is not already your practice, transitioning your prayer to two-way dialogue is life changing. A good practice is to offer heartfelt thanks, tell Him what is on your mind, and then be still and listen.

Although it might have been unfathomable during the introspective days of my youth, the truth is that the God of the universe not only knows everything about us, He is also interested in every last detail of our lives. We are told in Matthew 10:30 (NIV), "And even the very hairs of your head are all numbered." And He speaks directly to us with encouragement, direction, insight, and wisdom.

The more we truly let Him into the day-to-day, hour-to-hour moments of our lives, the closer we become. He longs for us to spend time with Him every day, loving Him like He loves us. It is truly life changing to know that our omnipotent Father is fully vested in us, loves us deeply, and holds us metaphorically in the palms of His hands. He lifts us up and catches us when we fall. He heals hearts and bodies.

As we totally commit ourselves and our lives to God, our intimacy grows even deeper. The more we figuratively die to ourselves in this world and dedicate our lives to Him, the deeper our joy.

The concept of "dying to ourselves" can alternatively be described as yielding to His will over our own will. God has a purpose and calling for each of our lives, which aligns with the unique attributes, gifts, and desires He has placed within us.

One of the best-selling books of all time—*The Purpose Driven Life*, by the aforementioned Rick Warren—broke new ground in helping millions and millions of people comprehend God's order and understand their unique calling. This book helps answer many of those introspective questions that swirled in my mind for so many years.

The notion of total commitment may sound scary, as we long for control over our lives, but it is the exact opposite. God intended for us to live in eternity, so understanding that this world is but a temporary staging ground changes your perspective. Beyond that, though, He is a good, good Father who knows the dreams placed in our hearts and yearns to bless us as we walk with Him.

Several months ago, Tara contemplated a job transfer to her company's London office. She had visited there the previous year and was deeply enamored with this European city. Surely, it was a major decision to leave the safety and comfort of family, friends, and familiar territory to establish herself in a new country, but the adventure captured her heart. The following essay speaks to that potential major life change, and ultimately, the peace and joy that comes from partnering with God.

Finding Peace Where You're Placed, by Tara

If you had spoken to me a year ago, if we had met for coffee to talk about life, I would have told you that I, in all seriousness, intended to move to London. I had already planned how I would put in a work transfer to our London office via an abroad program, and I had already decided which possessions I would sell, which I would beg my parents to keep at their home during my time away, and which special items would make the journey across the pond.

I had already spoken to knowledgeable friends about the best areas of town to reside in, and I had even perused flatmate-finder websites in my downtime. I read books and articles about the best places to eat, drink, and play in London; I researched the laws, language, and customs of the United Kingdom; and I anxiously awaited the day when I could once again find myself in the city that felt so mysteriously yet innately like home, like nowhere had before.

Honestly, even typing this all up now, a full year later, makes me feel a little bit queasy, like that sinking feeling in the pit of your stomach you get when you think about an ex or a dear friend you fell out of touch with. You see, I had planned my move to London down to every little, excruciating detail, yet I managed to disregard the largest component of it all: God's plan.

While it's perhaps a bit foolish, I think it's human nature to make plans and then expect those plans to work out flawlessly. Unfortunately, this isn't realistic. For a Christian, it is especially unrealistic, because such a large component of Christianity is trusting God and trusting His path for you. I don't know whether God has said no to London entirely, or if He has simply requested my patience, but I do know that my plan did not align with His.

It's human nature to want a blueprint. We want to sketch out our desires and color them to life. We want to write up a checklist and check off each item, one by one. We yearn for an itinerary, an outline, and a projection of the end result.

Can you imagine if God's plans for us were negotiable? Perhaps it would be like a business proposal. We'd say, "Hey, God, I have this really great idea and, with your approval, I think it will maximize your return on investment." And then God would either give us the stamp of approval or suggest an alternative—at which point, we could negotiate a middle ground. How great would that be, right?

But as wonderful as our proposed plans may seem at the onset, I think we would ultimately fail ourselves because our view is so limited. It's like asking the toddler in the car seat to be the eyes of the driver and safely navigate the vehicle on a winding road. Sure, we are independent creatures and able to make our own decisions (and mistakes) aplenty, but as

Christians, we have willingly given the wheel over to God. We've declared that we trust Him, and we've agreed to go along for the ride.

It's easier said than done, especially if you're inherently a control freak like me, but I've found there is a certain peace and calmness in letting go of your plans and trusting God's. If it were up to me, I wouldn't be where I am right now, but I have to believe that God has mindfully and purposefully planted me in the right place during the current season of my life. We can want, and dream, and pray, but ultimately, finding peace in where you've been placed is a beautiful thing.

A Deepened Relationship through Worship

Today, worship is often thought of as synonymous with Christian music, but it is really much more than that. Worship is really everything you do and how you go about doing it. Worship is a lifestyle.

Using another tree metaphor, Isaiah 61:3 (NKJV) speaks of God's children, "that they may be called oaks of righteousness, the planting of the Lord, that He may be glorified."

God created us in His own image for His pleasure. He has built us to experience pleasure ourselves, but ultimately He wants us to serve and praise Him.

Music surely is a great means to worship, particularly when it is sincerely intended to praise God. While doing this corporately at church or a concert can make us feel a tremendous closeness, it brings Him great pleasure for us to lift up songs of love and thanks.

Personally, I love worship music, and much of the backdrop of my days is filled with these sounds while I work, exercise, drive, pray, eat, and even sleep. I find the music and lyrics to be tremendously uplifting, stirring feelings of awe, appreciation, inspiration, peace, hope, love...and joy!

It serves as a constant reminder of God's goodness and presence and gives me a sense of connection throughout each day. Inevitably, no matter the circumstances, this music sparks a sense of joy. Additionally, bathing our minds and souls in these fragrant sounds and messages positively impacts how we interact with others and experience each day.

As good as this might be, worship really entails every way that we please God in how we carry out our lives, both large and small. Every time we make the right choice, smile at a stranger, offer help to another, provide words of encouragement, demonstrate patience, etc., etc., we engage in worship and make Him smile.

As friendship continues to develop, a deeper relationship might entail constant conversation throughout the day. He is a twenty-four-seven God, always there when we want to converse. We may not always hear back from Him, but you can rest assured that He is always listening and waiting to be called on.

At a recent conference, Jenn Johnson of Bethel Music stated it this way: "The minute you turn your thoughts to Jesus, He is there." Inviting Him into every aspect of your life moves toward worship. In *The Purpose Driven Life*, Rick Warren described it like this: "How is it possible to do everything to the glory of God? By doing everything as if you were doing it for Jesus and by carrying on a continual conversation with him while you do it."

It is important that we maintain consistency, communing with God and perpetuating a joyful heart of praise through all seasons and circumstances of our lives. Thanksgiving comes much more naturally in periods of abundance and prosperity, but choosing to be joyful and offering sincere praise during difficult periods might be the most powerful form of worship.

1 Thessalonians 5:16–18 (NLT) wraps this up very succinctly in a handful of words, saying, "Always be joyful. Never stop praying. Be thankful in all circumstances, for this is God's will for you who belong to Christ Jesus."

Rising above the immediate circumstances and allowing the long view to prevail in our hearts and minds is a tremendous act of faith. It blesses Him greatly when we recognize the rich blessings—past, present, and future—and rest in His hope and promise. Jeremiah 29:11 (NIV) very clearly assures us of this: "'For I know the plans I have for you,' declares the Lord, 'plans to prosper you and not to harm you, plans to give you hope and a future.'"

Living our lives with a heart of praise and thanksgiving brings joy to God. It also has an amazing reciprocal effect similar to gift giving. When we give gifts to others in love and they receive them with joy, we usually feel joy ourselves. Very similarly, when we bring joy to God through sincere praise, thanksgiving, or other acts of worship, our own heart typically is filled with joy.

Combining regular immersion in the Word with worship and an intimate relationship with God transforms our emotional state. It is as if our minds, bodies, and souls are recharged with vitality, peace, love, and joy.

CHAPTER 16
Partnering for Joy—a Match Made in Heaven

All Things for Good Testimony

As we near the conclusion of this collaborative book, it seems particularly relevant to share the somewhat unlikely paths we have journeyed to get here. Providing that backdrop helps to illustrate how God's ways are better than our ways and how He works all things for good.

At the outset of the book, I mentioned how a period of career transition several years ago afforded me the opportunity to pursue writing. This was a passion that was cultivated in high school and vigorously encouraged by the head of our English department, but I elected a different career path.

Throughout my lengthy career in the financial services industry, the embers of the dream to write more than correspondence and strategy documents continued to flicker and spark within me. When the right circumstances arose, I stepped into this passion by creating a blog and soon found myself serving as a featured columnist for a national sports media site.

Assignments, deadlines, quotas, feedback, and the sheer repetitive motion of cranking out article after article evolved and sharpened my skills. This period of growth became extremely valuable as I transitioned into a start-up marketing firm, which necessitated being involved with every last detail, including a great deal of copywriting.

I believed then that God blessed me with the opportunity to write and also allowed me to refine my skills for the next venture.

At the time, Tara was just beginning college, pursuing a major in journalism. From an early age, she demonstrated a passion and gift for writing, so it was not surprising when she elected to pursue this as her career.

As things would be, the timing was perfect for Tara to join our new business as a marketing intern in the summer before her sophomore year. She learned marketing, which interestingly became her second major, but spent a significant portion of her time copywriting.

Our time working together was a true blessing. It drew us closer and also allowed me to witness her talents in both areas. Tara landed in the advertising world out of college but continues to make time for writing and art on the side.

Although Beth did not get involved with our marketing business, she interestingly felt a calling from God to begin writing around this same time period and created her own blog. Her initial post, which appears below, explains the somewhat foreign pursuit and unlikely scenario that she launched into.

As I reflect back, although it was unseen by any of us at the time, it seems clear that God had a plan for all of us. He was working all things for good and according to a calling that He placed in each of our hearts.

This book serves as testimony to His goodness and marvelous ways. Who would have seen it coming—a banker and wannabe writer, a journalism major working in advertising, and a disinclined, latent writer coming together to publish a message of hope and joy.

Walk by Faith, Not by Sight, by Beth

"Walk by faith, not by sight"—a verse I have known since the beginning of my Christian walk.

"Walk by faith, not by sight"—a verse that I read in a devotional one day, and it resonated with me as only God's Word does when He is trying to reach you.

"Walk by faith, not by sight"—not directly referenced, but the message was clear, when my pastor spoke on this a few weeks later. It is that feeling you get when you are sitting in church and you feel as if God is speaking directly to you.

JOY ALL AROUND US

"Walk by faith, not by sight"—the verse I told my seventeen-year-old daughter one night as counsel for a situation troubling her.

"Walk by faith, not by sight"—a verse I could study until God calls me home, still not grasping all it means, yet also so simple to turn to for help in day-to-day life.

Walking by faith and not by sight, as God commands us to do in 2 Corinthians 5:7, means to live our life based on God's Word and His leading, not on the world as we see it. That is, trying to follow God's direction to us day by day and even minute by minute instead of being led by our thoughts, feelings, and emotions. As Romans 7:18 (NIV) reminds us, good itself does not dwell in us. Isaiah 64:6 (NIV) states it a bit stronger: "All our righteous acts are like filthy rags." When we allow ourselves to base our decisions in life on what we want or how we feel, the result will not be the best choice for our ultimate good or the good of those around us.

When Peter asked Jesus if he could come to Him on the water, he trusted in Jesus's answer, "Come." As he stepped out of the boat, his faith was in Jesus and His command, and he was able to do the impossible. When he started to look at the water and the circumstances around him instead of Jesus, he sank. In this story God has given us a real-life example of walking by faith. Just like Peter, our success as a Christ follower is based on our ability to carry out this command.

We have two paths we can choose in our life walk. One path is the world's way of living. The other path is following God's eternal truth. It is very easy to follow the world, the path we see. The world is telling us what to do, *loudly*, and our emotions are quick to jump in and tell us the world is right. God's eternal truth comes from a quieter but ultimately much stronger place, deep inside each of us, which is nurtured and made stronger by listening to His voice and studying His Word.

God is now calling me to start a journey that I am totally unqualified to handle. He is telling me, "Walk by faith, not by sight." When I publish this post, my journey begins. A journey I have no hope of completing on my own; only on the faith of His words do I dare take the first step. I need to step out of my boat and see what great things God will do as I walk by faith.

As we go through our lives, walking by faith and not by sight will be the more difficult choice to make. However, making those difficult choices to follow God's leading and not our own desires will always put us on the path to where God wants us to be. We need to ask ourselves, as Christians, isn't that where we know we belong?

Joy All around Us

There is no denying that there are many troubles in this world, and the trend line does not look favorable. The evolution of this world seems to be twisting more and more toward one that is backward and upside down.

Even so, we can position ourselves to live our lives in a way that changes our life experience.

Simply put, each of us has the ability to make choices that will evoke greater happiness and joy in our lives. When we transform our hearts and minds, we see the world and our lives differently. Our eyes train themselves on the blessings, and our minds embrace them.

As stated in the opening, our mission with this book is to help others recognize that this is within our grasp—and then show them how to reach out and secure it. We hope that the book has helped to shift your mindset at least a bit, but we would encourage you to place it on the coffee table or another prominent place to offer an ongoing grounding in the pathways to living joyously.

It would also be our great hope that you share the book with others. This is truly a case of the more, the merrier.

Joy really is all around us. Many simple choices we make allow us to access and experience it.

And the ultimate pathway is the joy of the Lord!

When we center our lives on God, we are able to get the best of both worlds. We attain the greatest level of joy when we partner with God—the Father, Son, and Holy Spirit! Together, we position ourselves for temporal happiness and sustaining joy.

Alternatively stated, some means are within our own human power, and others derive from His omnipresent, omnipotent power!

The great news is that it is all within our own power. It's simply a matter of prerogative to make these choices, including our relationship with God. He already chose us—we just need to choose Him!

It is our sincere, heartfelt desire for this book's message to lead many to enter into or deepen a relationship with Him to experience His great love and the joy that accompanies it.

Prayer for Joy

We would like to offer this closing prayer for every reader of this book:

Father,
  We love You and thank You for Your grace, mercy, and kindness.
  Thank You for being such a good, good Father, interested in every last detail of our lives.
  Thank You for Your enduring love and kindness, which exceeds even our wildest imaginations.
  Jesus, we thank You for Your tremendous sacrifice, the greatest act of love, to take away all our sins, shame, and sickness.
  We thank You for the gift of eternal life and for reconciling us with the Father.
  God, we ask for eyes to see You and ears to hear You.
  We thank You for the blessings You have poured out on us—help us to fully recognize and cherish them.
  Holy Spirit, we ask You to stir our hearts to seek, find, and deepen our relationship with the Lord, and with that, to experience His abundant peace and joy!
  In Jesus's name we pray.
  Amen.

One Final Testimony

Like many of you might feel, Beth and I have found ourselves on quite a journey over the past year. For us, that journey has involved me stepping away from my job that would have had us relocate to Atlanta.

This occurred for many reasons that I will not address here, but the upshot is that it has placed me in a period of transition to figure out what's next in my career. God has done some amazing things during this time period, and twenty-twenty hindsight has allowed us to see that we have actually been blessed with a sabbatical.

Of course, employment income is surely a good thing, but we have been blessed in so many other ways that far exceed any lost earnings. This has been a marvelous time of personal growth and life clarity grounded in the love of the Father, a sovereign Lord, and the guiding presence of the Holy Spirit.

We have experienced an almost total absence of anxiety through this "dry" period—and instead have experienced abundant peace and joy.

At the same time, Tara has been on her own somewhat separate journey. Although it does not entail unemployment, she is immersed in a major transition of her own, relocating to the Big Apple. She transferred from the more familiar southern environ of Atlanta to the urban bustle of New York City with the hope of a promotion. Her management career begins today as I key these words, which also brings financial blessing to overcome the already experienced jump in living costs.

A new job role, long walks and subway rides, less favorable weather, and the pace within the concrete confines of the sprawling metropolis surely will impose more adjustment and transition. Although this will bring some challenge, she will be served well by her spirit of adventure and zeal to pursue the good in every situation.

Just a few months prior to this transition, when contemplating a transfer across the pond to London, Tara wrote about finding peace where you're placed. Little did she know at that time she would be adjusting to the Empire City, the city that never sleeps.

God truly makes all things work together for good. As we have stepped forward in faith, we have literally watched Him make our paths straight. We may not see the path too far in front of us, but we keep on walking forward with trust. Chad Norris, senior pastor of Bridgeway Church in Greenville, South Carolina, recently offered this nugget of wisdom that spoke directly to my heart: "The Promised Land always becomes visible as we walk."

In other words, if we stand still, we might never get to the Promised Land. But as we move ahead in faith, partnering with God and centering ourselves on the limited path we see, we will begin to see His promise and plans before us. Walk by faith, not by sight.

The book that you hold in your hands serves as testimony to His goodness. It is truly a blessing that my newfound time could be redirected into, and that our family was afforded, the unique opportunity to collaborate on this initiative.

We also believe the circumstances provide powerful testimony to the overarching message of this book. During this period of potentially unsettling change and uncertainty, we could have been overridden with worry and anxiety. Instead, we have served as vehicles to put forth a message of hope and joy!

One Final Wish

Our own respective life journeys have demonstrated that we can find happiness and joy in many places around us. These emotions can be further enhanced and increased in frequency through the way we pursue life. Everything from the way we think to the people with whom we associate impacts our levels of happiness and joy.

Although we may not be able to directly conjure joy, we can be very intentional with our choices, mind-set, and surroundings to position ourselves to realize greater levels and frequency of this powerful emotion. Even so, periods of lower prosperity, difficulty, and challenge, like our family is currently experiencing, can dampen or altogether extinguish happiness and joy when we are missing the one enduring source—the joy of the Lord.

In closing, no matter what your individual circumstances may be, we encourage you to open your hearts, minds, and eyes to recognize the blessings and see the sources of joy in your own lives. Better yet, doing this with a life centered on and marked by a personal relationship with our unconditionally loving triune God leads to a pervasive, sustaining sense of joy deeply rooted within us.

As we have detailed within these pages, the pathway to joy does not require a long, arduous journey. Not only is it within our grasp, we hope that you will find that—*joy is all around us!*

Part 4
Finding the Ultimate Joy

CHAPTER 17
Salvation

Becoming Sons and Daughters of the Kingdom, by Beth

God wants nothing more than for you to become a member of His family, a citizen of His Kingdom. 1 Timothy 2:4 tells us God wants all men to be saved and come to the knowledge of truth. Before Adam and Eve sinned, God was with them. The Bible tells us He took walks with them during the cool of the day, just as an earthly father might do with his children. Can you imagine walking and talking with God? Although we cannot walk and talk with God as Adam and Eve did, when we join His family, our fellowship with Him is restored. God was not surprised when Adam and Eve sinned against Him. His plan was already in place to restore the fellowship with Him that was broken when sin entered the world.

If fellowship with your creator, the God of the universe, is something you are ready to step into, then continue reading. We will walk with you as you take this exciting step to become a member of God's family. Although we do not look to God as if He were a genie who makes wishes come true, He is a God who blesses those He calls His own. His Word is filled with promises for His children, promises for a blessed life here on earth, as well as the promise of being able to spend eternity with Him in Heaven.

Let's go to God's handbook for mankind, the Bible, where we can learn how to become His sons and daughters, and restore intimate fellowship with our Father.

When Jesus explained God's kingdom to a religious leader, He was very clear: "Very truly I tell you, no one can see the kingdom of God unless they are born again" (John 3:3 NIV).

Similarly, when a jailer where Paul and Silas were imprisoned asked them how he could be saved, they replied, "Believe in the Lord Jesus, and you will be saved" (Acts 16:31 NIV).

Christians use both these terms to talk about their decision to become members of God's family. Saying you are born again, or saved, really means you know who God is, and you know that without Him you are lost; that is, you recognize your need for a savior. In this position you are ready to surrender all to Him, and come under His Lordship for your life.

Now to get a bit more specific about what that means, we will look at Romans. This book was written by Paul for the church in Rome. The church in Rome was not started by Paul, and he wanted to encourage them, and teach them more about their new way of life.

In Romans 3:23 we learn that everyone falls short of God's standard: "all have sinned and fall short of the glory of God." In this same chapter, verse 10, Paul reminds us, "There is no one righteous, not even one."

Our sin separates us, all of us, from God. His perfect holiness cannot be in fellowship with sin. Romans 6:23 tells us that sin equals death: "For the wages of sin is death."

But God demonstrates his own love for us in this: while we were still sinners, Christ died for us.

Romans 5:8 (NIV) says, "Thankfully God had a perfect plan, through His son, to restore our fellowship with Him. Jesus who was son of man, and son of God, came to earth and lived a perfect life so he could offer himself as the sacrifice for our sins."

And 2 Corinthians 5:21 (NIV) states, "God made him who had no sin to be sin for us, so that in him we might become the righteousness of God."

Prayer is the door we step through to become part of His family. God made it so simple for us, and Jesus Christ did all the work for us. Jesus paid for all our sins, past, present, and future, through His sacrifice on the cross.

Romans 10:8-10 (NIV) instructs, "If you declare with your mouth, 'Jesus is Lord,' and believe in your heart that God raised him from the dead, you will be saved. For it is with your heart that you believe and are justified, and it is with your mouth that you profess your faith and are saved."

This is explained, "For it is by grace you have been saved, through faith—and this is not from yourselves, it is the gift of God—not by works, so that no one can boast" (Ephesians 2:8-9 NIV).

God brings everything to the table; we just have to accept His gift. In Psalm 34 we are told to taste and see that the Lord is good! Having walked in restored fellowship with Father God for over twenty years, I can say with all certainty, He is a good, good Father!

Before Jesus went to the cross, he explained to His followers that it was going to be better for them after He went away because He was going to send them the Holy Spirit. The Holy Spirit, the third part of our triune God, is the Spirit of God living within us. He is our counselor, comforter, and teacher. He leads us in the ways of the Father and helps us understand God's Word.

John 16:13 (NIV) tells us, "But when he, the Spirit of truth, comes, he will guide you into all the truth. He will not speak on his own; he will speak only what he hears, and he will tell you what is yet to come."

After Jesus' death and resurrection, He reminded them of this promise and told them to wait for the Holy Spirit to come to them.

> *On one occasion, while he was eating with them, he gave them this command: "Do not leave Jerusalem, but wait for the gift my Father promised, which you have heard me speak about. For John baptized with water, but in a few days you will be baptized with the Holy Spirit." (Acts 1:4—5 NIV)*

From all of the above verses, we can see it comes down to three key elements.

First, belief in our Creator, God, and recognizing that your sin separates you from Him. Second, accepting the paid work of Jesus's death on the cross to cleanse you from all unrighteousness so you can be reconciled with your Father. And lastly, confessing, or praying, to Him what is on your heart concerning these beliefs, and offering to Him your commitment to follow Him, and make Him Lord of your life.

Below is an example of a prayer to our Heavenly Father asking Him to bring you back where you belong, into His family. When you are ready you can pray this prayer, or speak from your own heart.

> *Father, You are the Creator of the universe, and my Creator too. I now understand that to restore fellowship with You I must confess my sins and turn away from my old ways of living toward You and Your ways for my life. Thank You, Jesus, for You have done it all! Through Your overwhelming love, which sent You to the cross, I am made righteous. Through Your willingness to pay the price for my sins with Your own life, I now can be welcomed into Father God's family and have fellowship with Him. Thank You, Jesus! I confess my sins and accept the forgiveness You have provided for me. I commit from this day forward to follow You. Father God, I make You Lord of my life. Holy Spirit, thank You for coming to live in me. Please lead and guide me in my new life as a member of God's family. Amen!*

Now that you have made this exciting decision, we encourage you to find a church family that is grounded in God's love and follows His Word. We also recommend you get a Bible and start to read and study about all God wants to share with you. Talk to Him often; He is always there and ready to listen to your prayers. If you have any questions, please contact us, as we would be happy to help you. Welcome to the family!

ADDITIONAL RESOURCES

- JoyAllAroundUs.com
    - Let us hear from you
        - Submit a review
        - Share a testimony and encourage others
        - Give us feedback or say hello
    - Purchase the book
        - Paperback (Grayscale)
        - Paperback (Full Color-Deluxe Version)
        - Kindle Versions
    - Give joy to others
        - Donate to the Spread the Joy! Program
        - Request bulk purchase discounts
    - Purchase related merchandise

- KingdomWinds.com
    - Join the Kingdom Winds Collective for Christian authors, artists, musicians and ministries
    - Experience the premier destination for God-inspired content
        - Fresh content produced by the talented Kingdom Winds Collective
        - Marketplace showcasing the creative works of the Kingdom Winds Collective
    - Value-added Support Services such as Publishing, Marketing, Web Design, and more
    - Visit KingdomWinds.com and KingdomWindsCollective.com to learn more and join

- Recommended Books
    - *Choose Joy* by Kay Warren
    - *The Purpose Driven Life* by Rick Warren
    - *Thrive: Digging Deep, Reaching Out* by Mark Hall
    - *Mama Jane's Secret* by Chad Norris

- TaraSuess.com
    - Original Art Designs
    - Commissioned Art Designs

DEDICATION

This book is dedicated to our Father, who chose us before the foundation of the world; Jesus, who died to give us abundant life; and the Holy Spirit, who guides us daily, is our constant source of joy, and inspired us to create this book. To God be the glory forever!

ACKNOWLEDGEMENTS AND CREDITS

Our lives have been touched, enriched and blessed with a wide array of joys, ranging from simple pleasures to the supernatural. We have shared many of them throughout this book, detailing these heartfelt and intimate memories and experiences.

We offer our sincere appreciation and love to everyone, past and present, who have contributed to and shared these joys with us. Family members (including our furry ones,) friends, faith leaders, co-workers, teammates, teachers, mentors, classmates, acquaintances, and even strangers—some named and some unnamed within the book—have been integral to our journeys and the joys that have blessed our lives.

Specifically, we would like to recognize Jack and Amonda Hancock, who have been both friends and spiritual leaders over the past eighteen months. Their prayers and prophesy have provided, more than they likely even know, much inspiration and encouragement through the journey of creating our first book.

It would probably be safe to assume that in reading this book, you have deduced that the feline members of our household have offered us much joy through the years. Like most families, it can often be difficult to find complete, unanimous agreement on specific matters—but this is one sentiment that each of us is in absolute agreement. And, as described in *Twins of Different Mothers* in Chapter Twelve, Pippa has provided particular inspiration in writing this book with the palpable joy that she radiates everyday.

In closing, we thank our wonderful, loving God for placing the passion to write this book on our hearts, and the ongoing inspiration to allow it to become reality. He has been by our side to lead and encourage us through this collaborative effort from start to finish.

AUTHOR BIO

A collaborative effort between a husband, wife, and daughter, this book is based on their real-life journeys.

Gary spent the majority of his career as an executive in the financial services industry. He's also written for a national sports website as a featured columnist. His career, family and friends, varied passions, and personal faith journey have all influenced his perspective on a joyful life.

After a banking career, Elizabeth transitioned her focus to raising their daughter, managing the household, engaging in women's ministry, and caring for their beloved cats. She has nurtured her passion for writing through blogging, centering on helping others navigate unpredictable life journeys.

After graduating from the University of South Carolina with a degree in Advertising and concentration in Journalism, Tara currently works for a large advertising agency as a Media Planner. On the side, she maintains a burgeoning career as an artist, offering custom, commissioned artwork along with many original creations of her own design available on TaraSuess.com and KingdomWinds.com.

www.ingramcontent.com/pod-product-compliance
Lightning Source LLC
Chambersburg PA
CBHW071303110426
42743CB00042B/1151